DATE DUE			
MR 29 88			

HOW TO BE AN ANTIQUES DETECTIVE

HOW TO BE AN ANTIQUES DETECTIVE

by
Anne Gilbert

GROSSET & DUNLAP
A FILMWAYS COMPANY
Publishers • New York

457 9371

9-18-78 Baker 9-49

To my family—antiques detectives of the future

Acknowledgments

My thanks to Robert S. Ramsay, Jr. for his photographs of the Chicago Art Institute Oriental Arts, the Malcom Dunn Hudson River School Paintings, and the Joseph Fell Oriental Rug collection; also to John Keefe, Curator, Oriental Decorative Arts, The Art Institute of Chicago; Olga Sorensen Fuss; Gwen Trindl; James Zipprich; Jane Ryden; Malcom Dunn; Joseph Fell; Oscar Getz; James Bartells; James Williams; Dr. Thomas Ziebold; Chase Gilmore of Chicago Art Galleries; Campbell Museum Collection; Wilmette Library; Maggie Warden.

Contents

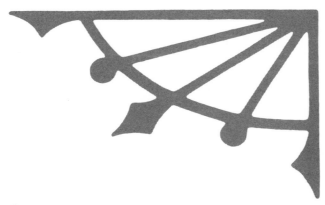

Introduction

In solving a problem of this sort, the grand thing is to be able to reason backward.

—Sherlock Holmes,
in *A Study in Scarlet*

Just what is it that makes the whole antique collecting scene so exciting when you'd think everything is already owned or overpriced? It's the element of chance that drives collectors in search of that ten thousand dollar item priced at one hundred dollars.

But is it sheer luck when you buy a Shaker rocker in-the-rough for a couple of dollars or a rare oil painting for seven dollars? At the same time and same place where these actual items were passed up by hundreds of so-called experts and dealers, they were found by an "antiques detective." No, more than luck added them to someone's collection—good detective work did it. Those objects offered clues that clicked in the sleuth's mind as "rare oil painting" and "fine Shaker chair." The antiques detective saw what the expert didn't because she had done research, had patience, and, to be sure, enjoyed a generous soupçon of luck.

The antiques detective doesn't accept objects at their face value—because an object bears a label proclaiming it as vintage doesn't automatically make it an antique. A good detective looks for clues and characteristics that will prove to his or her satisfaction the authenticity of the piece. He can ignore the so-called experts because he will use instead the tools of his trade to analyze the various clues which are to be found.

None of the antiques detectives I know will accept the mantle of expert, even lightly laid upon their shoulders. They often confess that they don't know any real experts in the antiques world. I don't. However, I do know many collectors, dealers, and curators who are as knowledgeable as you can

1

get. Yes, some of our best friends are dealers—those who can admit to being wrong on occasion. All admit to having goofed on some of their purchases, just as I have. It's through experience, including an occasional error, that we all learn.

By now you may have an idea of why many people find the detecting approach to collecting so appealing. They have the whole antique world to pick and choose from. They can buy from dealers, auction houses, house or garage sales and flea markets. Some, as you'll learn, even do very well in antique shops, much to the dismay of the dealers who then find out that they had a rare object lying around, unrecognized and underpriced. Whose fault is it if the dealer lets a good antique get away? On the other hand, objects are sometimes sold (and priced!) as antiques when they really aren't. Dealers aren't necessarily trying to fool you intentionally—they just don't have the time to research every item they buy. When something purchased from another dealer comes into the shop, its label is accepted as correct. Perhaps it is labeled "Peking glass," when it may or may not be Peking. An error can be compounded as the object goes from hand to hand. The antiques detective must make his own decision as to whether or not a piece is as labeled.

By the time you have completed my course in becoming an antiques detective, I hope you will be eager to try your own detecting methods. Or you may just decide to forget the whole thing, as being too much work! It is certainly easier to accept the word and opinion of others who seem to know more. And should you accept the challenge to do your own detecting, you'll find scoffers waiting to call you a variety of names, even "liar." Because they haven't found the rarities you have, they don't believe that it's possible. Never mind. Like your real-life counterpart, you have to get used to taking chances. Polish up your magnifying glass, dust off your library card and museum memberships. Mystery, danger and intrigue lie ahead for the antiques detective.

1.
What It Takes to Be an Antiques Detective

Not invisible, but unnoticed, Watson. You did not know
where to look, and so you missed all that is important.
                                    —SHERLOCK HOLMES,
                        in *The Adventures of Sherlock Holmes*

The lightning zigzagging across the pitch black sky cast eerie shadow-fingers on the Gothic mansion. While claps of thunder boomed, an unrelenting rain dropped on a curving line of umbrellas. Grim-faced, silent men and women waited in the dampness. Occasionally they shifted from one foot to the other. Were they waiting to pay their last respects to the deceased inside the decaying house? On the contrary, they were waiting to pick clean the bones of the dearly departed's possessions.

Scattered amongst the crowd were antique dealers, collectors, curiosity seekers and at least one antiques detective. This was no ordinary estate sale. The sagging house and its varied contents had belonged to a well-known, ninety-year-old widow. In her earlier years she had been famous for her wit, beauty and antiques. Though it would be nice to relate she had died peacefully in her sleep, she had been the unfortunate victim of a grisly murder. The motive, of course, had been robbery. Missing were her jewels and a valuable collection of *objets d'art*. Even so, there remained many antiques for the grasping hands of eager buyers. Were they upset that some blood stains had not been removed from the Oriental rugs? Not so you would notice. Were they unnerved that one of the antique swords now for sale had been used to skewer the victim? Heavens no! After all, they were for the most part professional dealers, used to cleaning antique carcasses and to participating in a little bloodletting among themselves.

Suddenly the scarred doors, swollen from the rain, creaked open. Just as

Ever the skeptic, the antiques detective will look at this seven-inch bottle and observe that while the engraving technique could date it as 18th century, the shape and manner of manufacture point to 19th century. Is it American or European? The copper-wheel-engraved floral motif could indicate either origin. Is it a cologne or a medicine bottle? The shape says it could be either.

suddenly, umbrellas snapped shut and the crowd came alive. Pushing and jostling, they surged through the doors in a hard core of "fifty first."

Objects were grabbed from tables and shelves in a silent frenzy. Quite a few were stolen. Oriental rugs were quickly rolled and hoisted over shoulders. In a matter of minutes the experts had gone in straight to the kill and stripped the house of hundreds of objects. With such scant time to study their purchases, did they know what they were buying? Had they known before the doors opened what was where? As quickly as they had scooped up almost everything in sight, the first fifty paid and rushed out the front doors. Could anything possibly be left for the others still waiting in the rain? Wouldn't the dealers have spotted all the best antiques and have left nothing behind but broken pottery and chairs without legs?

As box upon box of antiques were carried out, some of the waiting crowd became discouraged and left, but not the antiques detectives. In fact, they appreciated the chance to take their time and anticipated the challenge of looking over what the army of experts had left behind.

As one of those antiques detectives I was delighted to drip dry and casually walk past the denuded shelves and bare rooms. In one almost completely cleaned-out china cabinet I spotted a seven-inch-high clear glass bottle. Its price tag was five dollars. The ground glass stopper was in perfect condition, as was the bottle. Examining the bottle, I noted the floral design engraved on it. Turning it upside down, I saw a design cut into the base: a series of raised lines, radiating from the center. On the basis of these two clues I came to the conclusion that it was an early-19th-century cologne bottle. The style of the engraving was done with a copper wheel, then acid-etched, in the manner of Early American Stiegel glass. The chains of flowers were similar to motifs used by Baron Von Stiegel in his glassworks. However, the bottle also resembled some glassware made by the Boston & Sandwich Company in the 19th century. I believed the piece to be a mid-19th-century bottle, either from one of the New England glass houses or from Europe. I didn't mind at all that the bottle had been passed up by professional dealers. As an antique detective I had the courage of my convictions. Where others saw merely a glass bottle, old "eagle eyes" recognized important and obvious clues. It was a matter of knowing what to look for and where.

Knowing what to look for can make or break an antiques detective, as well as save valuable time. Instead of asking a nearby dealer or seller if the object looks like an authentic what's-it, the antiques detective will zip out her jewelers loup or magnifying glass and scrutinize the object. If it is, for instance, a would-be Currier & Ives print, the quickie examination will reveal telltale dots that would mark it a reproduction or "restrike."

Courage, a most important qualification, enables the average collector to overcome the kind of dealer intimidation that we all have probably experienced at least once. Remember when you spotted what looked like a fine carved primitive of a chicken? Foolishly, you asked the opinion of the nearest dealer. He probably hadn't even noticed it before. "That? Why, it is obviously something done by a child. Probably in woodworking class," he

The base offers another clue to the age of the bottle. The "diamond-rayed" design base was a pattern of the Boston & Sandwich Company, in the mid-19th century. However, other American glass houses adopted Sandwich base patterns.

sneered. Feeling totally worthless and ignorant you put it down. While you furtively looked around and hoped no one else had seen you pick it up, the dealer bought that fine American primitive for a couple of dollars. You'll find it later in his shop for several hundred. This intimidation can undermine the confidence of even the most experienced antiques collector. All of us have been conditioned to believe that the dealer—any antique dealer—knows more than we do, no matter if we have studied our own collections for years and have become more truly expert on the subject than the majority of dealers. But courage can keep the antiques detective from accepting certain misconceptions that have been handed down from generation to generation. Let's say you are a pewter collector. One day your research turns up some information that causes you to re-examine your entire collection and to question the dealer who sold some of the pieces to you, especially since he professed to be an expert on the subject. It may only be a sentence or two in a book that starts you thinking, such as: "The weight of a piece can often identify Britannia posing as pewter; it was the custom to add body to the thin sheets of Britannia by wrapping them around an iron core." Checking over your pewter collection, you discover that some of the expensive pieces purchased from the specialist-dealer are actually Britannia (an alloy made to resemble pewter in the middle and later 19th century). The next time you go to that dealer's shop, you carefully examine the so-called early pewter for the additional heaviness and other characteristics that might indicate Britannia. (Britannia and pewter are both variable alloys made up mainly of iron. While most Britannia also contains antimony and copper,

This chalice with the touchmark of James Dixon & Sons has the classic shape of early pewter. Would you turn it down if you learned it is classified as Britannia instead? Made around 1830, it wasn't affected by later Victorian designs.

What It Takes to Be an Antiques Detective 7

pewter is mainly tin. Britannia is always heavier than pewter. You can often recognize Britannia by its silvery look and by its paneled and fluted shapes. Because it was spun, it could be made into a variety of shapes and curves not possible in pewter.) Being a good-natured soul, you give the dealer a second chance by asking innocently why some of his goblets are heavier than others. Since you can hardly wait to share your new-found knowledge with the friendly dealer, imagine your surprise when the dealer is transformed into a snarling werewolf who doesn't agree with your findings. Thus begins the battle of intimidation. As a dealer with a reputation for expertise, he must insist on the correctness of his opinions. You'd better know everything there is to be learned about pewter and match him fact for fact. This courageous refusal to be intimidated by the dealer separates the antiques detective from the average collector. It also allows the antiques detective to stand up to the obnoxious fellow collector who must always be right. His misinformation has probably been handed down from various dealers and he has docilely accepted their opinions as the final word. His mind long ago slammed shut on any new information. Actually, what is so bad about Britannia? Thomas Danforth Boardman of Hartford, Connecticut, a pioneer in Britannia making, made teapots beginning in 1806. His eagle mark is found on those teapots.

Curiosity and an open mind lead the antiques detective to question constantly why, how, and when objects were made. This same curiosity also turns up many clues that can distinguish the true from the false antique. For example, a collector might question an armchair supposedly made in England in the middle 18th century. At least before the collector pays the asking price, he should make a careful review of the chair's features. His first question would be: Is the design in keeping with the period? Why does it have Shaker-type finials and slats, Queen Anne feet and smoothly turned stretchers? His curiosity will prompt him to take a look at those turnings with his magnifying glass. Research will have taught him to recognize that these particular turnings were done on a power lathe, unknown two hundred years ago. His familiarity with wood grains makes him aware of the fact this particular chair is made of cherry, while this type was usually made of maple. His deduction will be that the chair is an attempt to imitate a bannister-back chair of the type made between 1700 and 1725. An uninformed collector might have thought he'd stumbled on a rarity not pictured in any book, rather than a fake in a hodgepodge of styles.

As you can see, often the mystery is not how old a piece is, but whether such a piece ever existed before this year.

The same open mind that helps you question phony chair details will help you admit when you've made a mistake. Why did you buy that Currier & Ives restrike when you should have known better? By recognizing and retracing the reasons for the error, the antiques detective lessens the chance of making the same mistake twice.

Déjà-vu, or "I have seen this before," regularly happens to the true antiques detective. It results from a knowledge that is a combination of seeing, touching and reading about the objects collected. Don't confuse it with intuition: that's a whole other scene. *Déjà-vu* tells you at twenty paces that the blue and white porcelain dish is early Japanese Arita, not Chinese Export. You have seen that shade of blue, that shape of bowl before. Perhaps it was in a museum. The facts and features recorded in your subconscious practically jump into view beside the physical dish or bowl. Without your even picking it up and turning it over for close examination, *déjà-vu* tells you that you have seen the object before. It can also trigger your memory of a familiar piece once found to be fake.

THE BELLE OF NEW YORK.

The seller claimed to have found this Currier & Ives charmer in the lid of an old trunk. It is properly faded and with some brown age stains. The antiques detective will ignore the story and look for the facts. Under a loup or magnifying glass, small dots emerge that show the print is an original. Larger wide-spaced dots would have meant a restrike.

Not asking for advice is a hard habit for any antiques collector, even the antiques detective, to form. When you ask another person for his opinion of an object, you assume that he is an expert and you aren't. Regardless of how innocent or casual the question, asking it is a no-no. Wouldn't it be lovely if you could ask a fellow collector or dealer a simple question and get a simple answer? It doesn't happen in the antique world. Fellow collectors tend to be a little jealous of another's discoveries. Their tendency is to downgrade the object rather than to give a simple answer. But look at it from their point of view. Why should you discover a handwrought iron spatula for fifteen dollars when they have just paid fifty for a similar one?

Because you want reassurance that what you are pouring your tea from really is a 19th-century Rockingham teapot, you trot off to your friendly antique dealer who specializes in American primitives and country pieces. After you pay him a small stipend for his time and knowledge, he states positively that the piece isn't from Bennington or very old. He thinks that the teapot was probably made in the 1920's and sold in the five-and-ten. Not satisfied, you then take the piece to a posh auction house that often puts Bennington pottery on the block. The expert there proclaims the piece to be English Rockingham, 19th-century and "very nice." *Very nice* is often used when the expert doesn't know anything about an object and doesn't want to hurt the owner's feelings by telling him the piece is "a dog." A little confused, you consult the local museum curator, who beams with pleasure and proclaims the piece "obviously late-19th-century, probably made in one of

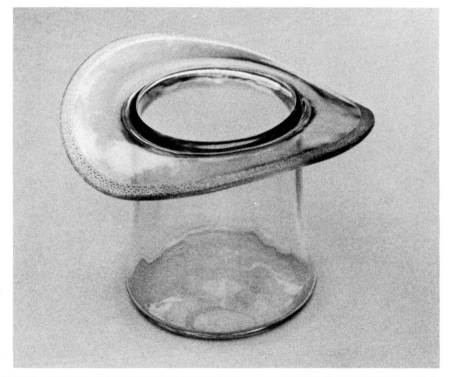

This blown-glass Victorian whimsey in the shape of a hat is a reproduction. But if you didn't know, would you buy it for four dollars anyway? The antiques detective would examine the pontil first. The pontil mark doesn't look the way it should when made by hand. It looks pressed in, a technique used by 20th-century fakers. Ignore the tiny bubbles in the glass. An even more important clue is the design on the rim of the hat, mold-etched—a strictly automated process. Many pieces of Depression Glass have similar mold-etched designs. The pattern or design was etched or cut into the mold to simulate the look of hand etchings. A little déjà-vu *can help here, too. Haven't you seen this type of design before, on some pieces of 1930's glassware?*

the United States Midwest potteries." He shows you a similar piece enshrined in the museum and suggests a book on the subject. Finally, doing just what you should have done in the first place, you go to the library and begin plowing through every available book on the subject of Rockingham, Bennington and early American yellowware. And what do you know? You spot an almost identical piece pictured in one of the books, captioned, "made in Peoria, Illinois, turn of the century." The book points out certain characteristics that show why this piece is typical of those made in Peoria at that time. The value of your piece has now become of secondary importance. You've gotten a taste of what it means to be an antiques detective and how to go about forming your own opinions by sifting facts. Whether the teapot is of less value because it was made in Peoria and not in Bennington really doesn't matter at this point. What is important is that you have discovered many types of pottery similar to Bennington wares were made in many places in the 19th and early 20th centuries. This is only the beginning of building a collection that may expand beyond the limits of objects made in one factory. And you have taken the first steps towards being an antiques detective. Next time, when you spot a similar piece, you'll ask yourself, "What makes this Peoria, Galena, or Bennington? What are the clues?"

Intuition can be a temporary substitute for later knowledge. When a snap judgement must be made, intuition can turn up a spectacular antique find. Just ask any antiques hunter who has fought her way through the house or estate sale melee how important intuition is. Her eyes will light up as the

Here are two pieces of Rockingham to confuse an antiques detective. The teapot on the left was molded in one piece—handle and spout. The raised circle design is indistinct, as is the acorn top on the lid. Even though the underpart of the base is unfinished, the piece appears to have been made around 1900, perhaps for one of the early Sears Catalogs. The piece on the right gives evidence of being handmade. The handle is applied and the turning marks still show faintly on the inside. The brown and yellow mottling is handsome and even though the pitcher is short and squat, it is, overall, pleasingly primitive. Neither piece has any maker marks. Some museum-hopping might turn up helpful clues to identity.

collector tells about the Britannia chalice she spotted across the crowded room, or about the Zanesville bottle or early painted tin tray. Perhaps the lady didn't know much about Britannia or pewter without her book on touchmarks. Nevertheless, intuition told her that twenty dollars for the chalice was a good price. Her magnifying glass showed the piece was made by James Dixon & Sons. James who? Not till she got home and began researching, did she discover the piece had been made in the early 19th century in England. Not quite pewter and finer than the usual Britannia alloy, it turned out to be early Britannia. Flipping through a price guide and reviews of recent auction prices, she learned the chalice would probably sell for between seventy-five and one hundred twenty dollars. If she had hesitated because she knew nothing about James Dixon, she would have passed by an interesting addition to a pewter collection. Intuition is well worth listening to when an object doesn't cost more than a few dollars. It is also useful for assessing such items as the Zanesville bottle and the painted tin tray. Surprisingly enough, the usual collector of bottles doesn't easily recognize an early Zanesville flask. One reason is that he doesn't expect to find one. These early-19th-century American bottles don't often surface at house and garage sales. The shock of seeing one for a couple of dollars, when its market value is over four hundred dollars, can cause disbelief. But the true antiques detective won't hesitate to plunk down a couple of dollars when intuition tells her this is a Zanesville flask and logic says "t'ain't so." There will be plenty of time to check out the bottle once it is safely at home. And if intuition proves wrong, it still will make an interesting flower holder.

A system or technique has to be developed to "psych out" antiques. The antiques detective has to change the way he views an object. It should first be seen as a simple shape. Take, for example, a chest of drawers. Draw an outline of the piece on paper. Later, you'll be able to draw it in your mind's eye. Leave out the hardware, color, and any other "filler" details. What do you see? Begin with the feet and work your way up. The chest pictured on this page shows front feet to be bracketed, with scroll-cut corner skirts. Your immediate deduction would be that the chest is Chippendale style. Next look at some of the details. The drawer pulls are carved fruit of the type done in the late Victorian period. The drawers are trimmed with decorative burl veneers, another feature of Victorian furniture. The keyholes are applied wood circles, yet another Victorian touch. The graining of the wood shows it to be walnut. (See page 18 to learn how to distinguish wood types.) By now your deduction would be that the chest is middle- to late-19th-century Victorian-style. At this point you have two conflicting deductions, both based only on the front exterior of the chest.

Now examine the back of the chest, with its features filled in. The wide, unevenly cut boards are unfinished. Saw marks are circular. If you are a collector of American furniture, you are aware that the circular saw came into general use in this country after 1830. But is the chest American?

Next remove the drawers and examine them. They are double-dovetailed (front and back) and made of pine. An examination of the drawer lock shows

Just for fun, take a piece of thin paper and trace the outline of this chest. Don't fill in the details. It looks like a country piece with adaptations of Chippendale styling in the bracket foot and scalloped apron corners. Outline the piece again to indicate the back of the chest. Draw three wide vertical lines. If you made a deduction at this point, you would say the chest was made around 1800. Now draw some curved arc lines across the "back" and pretend they are saw marks. By these simple strokes of your pen, your piece now dates from 1830. The antiques detective would deduce that the "frills" were added at a later date. The trim and drawer pulls were in fashion towards the end of the 19th century. The piece began as a transition piece with late-18th-century influences carried over to the end of the first quarter of the 19th century.

that it isn't handwrought iron. In fact, there is a scooped-out piece of wood under the lock. Behind the fruit drawer pulls are mismatched single holes.

On the basis of this evidence we feel confident in deducing that the chest was made in the early part of the 19th century, after 1830. The moulding and drawer pulls were added at a later time in an attempt to keep up with the current decorating fashions. The locks were also added later and changed to conform with the prevailing styles. Because the piece is unsophisticated, you can assume that it was a country craftsman's attempt to copy the Chippendale style. The original drawer handles were probably brass or wooden knobs, which accounts for the single holes behind the existing fruit handles. This "psyching out" enables you, the antiques detective, to arrive at a solution to the mystery of your antique through a series of logical deductions.

Until you get used to envisioning objects in outline form, practice on paper. Gradually you'll be able to tell when a piece of furniture has been altered (changed from a larger piece to a totally different, smaller object) and what if any pieces have been added since the piece was originally made. Most antiques detectives are able to say, "It just doesn't look right." What they mean is that there is something wrong with the outward appearance, from decorations not in keeping with the period to mismatched design elements.

These days the mystery is often not how old a piece is but when it was first reproduced. There are so many antique reproductions around, that detecting the more expensive frauds has become a full-time business for some people. The ultimate antiques detective in this area may be Dr. Thomas Ziebold, President of Braddock Services, Inc., of Gaithersburg, Maryland. He has parlayed his background in nuclear materials into a career of detecting art frauds. His clients range from museums to private collectors. It becomes a battle between the methods of science and the skill of the faker. "The scientists looks at art with a variety of instruments for measuring the physical and chemical properties of the object. With the proper selection of scientific procedures, any forgery may be detected through inconsistencies of materials, age or artist's technique," Ziebold says. He asks himself, "If I were to fake such a piece, what would I do?" Like any good antique detective, he may study a single piece for a day or two under a microscope (you would probably use a magnifying glass). This enables him to focus on such suspicious things as patina, cracks caused by fakers of ancient pottery, who drop them to simulate the old naturally cracked pieces. Under ultraviolet light, new cracks show up. Ziebold's newest detection method, known as TLD (thermoluminescent-dosimetry), dates inorganic materials such as pottery. He uses X-rays to detect alterations in antique silver, where the technique can show up recent soldering; a desirable hallmark from a small piece may be soldered onto a larger piece to make it appear more valuable.

Dr. Ziebold points out that his tests, which measure exposure to radiation, work only on objects made before the 19th century. In case you are thinking of dashing to the laboratory with your favorite ivory Netsukè, hold off! The carbon-14 test that determines the age of ivory requires burning a large hunk of the ivory. And the doctor advises collectors that two of the most often faked objects, jade pieces and pre-Columbian figures, can't be tested by his methods. That is good news for the crooks who are busily grinding them out.

But don't be discouraged. You can develop some scientific tests at your own collecting level, with some simple household tools forming your basic detection kit. These tools are: a magnifying glass and/or jeweler's loup, measuring tape, flashlight, magnet, and black-light bulb.

A good home reference library is a must for an antiques detective. This doesn't mean spending a fortune on books. Instead, concentrate on building up a library of special catalogs. These would include auction house catalogs announcing significant auctions, along with photographs of the items for sale. You'll find lists of such catalogues in various antique trade publications. A superb catalog is put out by Sotheby Parke Bernet for every one of their big auctions. Hundreds of items that the antique collector might not be familiar with are pictured, described and given estimated prices. To get on their mailing list for press information on future auctions, write them at 980 Madison Avenue (Seventy-Sixth – Seventy-Seventh Streets) New York, New York 10021. Their catalogs also explain auction terms and the descriptive terms (in the style of Chippendale, etc.). After the individual auctions have been held, you may send for the final bid sheets. What could be more helpful for the antiques detective trying to get an idea of what his collection is currently worth? Keep in mind, though, that prices for the same type of object will vary in different parts of the country. Early American objects will command higher prices in the East, while golden oak and Victorian pieces are more popular in Nebraska or Missouri.

Catalogs from the large art and historical museums are printed for their important exhibitions. If the subject is one that interests you, such as Art Nouveau or French furniture, you'll find accurate descriptive information and photographs. Many of the items on exhibition are on loan from private collections. Therefore, these catalogs offer the antiques detective a reference source to objects not always described in the usual books.

From time to time special booklets on a single subject are printed by curators of museums. When they first come out, they are advertised in the magazine *Antiques*. After that, you'll find them only in museum book stores.

Often antique dealers who have seriously collected and specialized in one type of antique will put out paperback booklets on their own. One good example is antiques dealer Elinor Gordon, whose little booklet, *Oriental Lowestoft*, explains away a lot of myths about Chinese Export porcelain. You can obtain one by writing to Elinor Gordon, P.O. Box 211, Villanova, Pennsylvania 19083. Even the State Department has published illustrations and descriptions of some important American antiques in a *Guidebook to Diplomatic Reception Rooms*. You can get it for two dollars (unless the price has gone up) from The Fine Arts Committee, Department of State, Washington, D.C. 20520.

Other good reference sources are the various antique trade magazines and newspapers. You can learn a lot from the research of specialized collectors and curators who write for the trades. Some antiques detectives buy the special heavy binders offered by the various publications to keep the material indexed and neatly at hand.

One antiques detective I know enjoys thumbing through the magazines, trying to figure out from the clearly-detailed photographs which of the Georgian antiques are genuine and which are new. Seeing if you can detect which pieces are "hot off the assembly line" is great entertainment for a rainy day and good practice.

A good antiques detective needs to know what different types of woods look like. Can you tell curly maple from birdseye? Pine from birch? You'd be surprised how many would-be antiques detectives don't know a burl from an oyster. Burl is a growth on such trees as maple, walnut and ash. It was used for decorating furniture and also turned into some mighty valuable and handsome treenware bowls. Oystering is the diagonal cutting of the wood to show the grain in a pattern similar to that of an oyster. If you can recognize burl, you may be able to spot a dusty treenware bowl that others have passed by. The two turned bowls (next page) were purchased at different house sales for two dollars apiece. One was lying on the floor of a basement. The other was atop a cupboard with two different kinds of bowls nested inside it.

Warping is a thing of beauty, when it is part of treenware aging. These two handmade wooden bowls were overlooked at housesales, because they were drab and uninteresting. They had a dried-out appearance from neglect and age. Several days of oiling restored their rich wood graining. The very thing that turns off an antiques hunter will turn on the antiques detective. Remember, the warping is an important clue.

You can spot clues to age when the bowls are turned upside down. Both show the concentric lines of hand-turning on a lathe. The turned-over lip is another clue. The bowl on the right shows how its maker took advantage of the wood grain to achieve an oystering effect.

Here's a good example of "oystering." In this case, the veneers have been applied to a small table top.

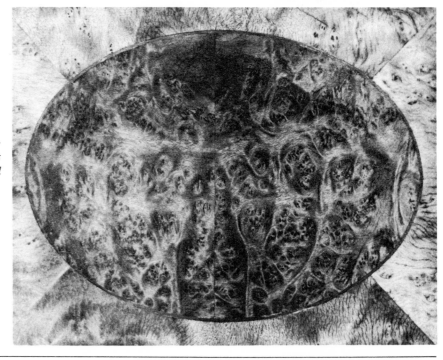

Mail away for some wood samples to familiarize yourself with the look of various wood grains and colors. Top to bottom left: redwood burl; white gum; walnut crotch; cherry. Top to bottom right: striped satinwood; Zebra wood; white birch; teak. Since many woods are to be found only in certain countries or were used by specific countries for certain types of furniture, knowing woods and their origins will offer valuable clues.

The first thing about a treenware bowl would be its irregular, warped shape. Closer inspection might reveal oystering. Even though both of these bowls first appeared drab and uninteresting, a good rubdown with salad oil for several days brought out the beauty of their hand-turning.

To learn the characteristics of the various woods, mount a set of small samples on a board and refer to them often. A source for samples is Craftsman Wood Service Company, 2727 South Mary Street, Chicago, Illinois 60608. Their mail-order catalog also lists supplies for restoring antique wood pieces, from veneers to inlays.

The ability to recognize the marks of old tools can help you unmask many antique reproductions, and help put real antiques in their historical context. If you are sincere about becoming an antiques detective, you will have to learn how objects were made two hundred years ago. If there is one tool whose mark is a common denominator in dating wood, brass, pewter, some silver and ceramics, it is the hand-turned wood lathe. Used for finishing and smoothing objects, it left behind valuable clues. Objects turned slowly by hand on the lathe more than one hundred years ago will still show coarse, concentric rings. Look again at the undersides of the two treenware bowls. Their rings, still visible today, are important clues to the age of the bowls. Today's fast-turning lathes leave no pressure marks and so create a smooth finish. Next time you find a piece of furniture with wooden knobs or rungs that were turned, check them with your magnifying glass. If they were made

This small chamberstick offers myriad clues to the observant antiques detective. The concentric lines denoting turning on an early lathe are easy to see. Notice the rough, almost sharp turning on the lip of the saucer, another good indication of hand turning. The piece comes apart, and the screws also are crude and hand-wrought. Judged by these clues and the beautiful ring when it is tapped, the antiques detective concludes that the piece was made early in the 19th century. It has no marks and since few American brass workers put their stamp on their pieces, it is quite possibly American.

on an old, hand-turned lathe, those concentric lines will probably still show. Unless it has been worn down with age, some antique silver hollow ware will show similar marks. If you think you have an authentic antique pewter charger or plate, look across the skimming marks on the bottom. There should be coarse radial lines extending from the circumference. Known as "chatter" marks, they were caused by the vibration of the skimming tool and are evidence of age. Those antique pieces made on primitive lathes with wooden bearings will show coarser markings than will modern pieces.

Do those brass candlesticks with the label saying "18th-century British" show lathe marks or other clues of age? Spun brass will have minute concentric rings running around it, as will molded brass candlesticks placed on the lathe for smoothing. However, lathe marks may not always be the final clue. Some modern pieces may show lathe marks and others will even be done in the old way by skilled craftsmen who demonstrate the old techniques to museum visitors.

Marks left by early saws are important clues to the age of furniture. The antiques detective will learn to recognize the jagged kerf marks of a frame or pit saw from the 17th or 18th century (and early 19th). On pieces made after 1830 he will expect to find circular marks left by the circular saw. And his 18th-century chest should not have the straight lines made by today's band saw.

To identify glassware, you must learn to recognize the telltale marks left by the glassblower which record each improvement in the making of glass. History books on the development of glass are a good place to start. When you know what ingredients were used for early glass, you can recognize the look, weight, and sometimes the sound of it.

If a piece is said to have its original painted surface, the antiques detective has to decide if this is true. A thorough knowledge of colors and the characteristics of paint will offer clues. It is easy to see if the paint comes off in big chips or shows a thick texture where some has flaked off. Almost every soft wood was liable to be decorated, but walnut and mahogany, expensive and "showy" in their day, were not covered by paint. Therefore, if the antiques detective comes across a piece of furniture of walnut or mahogany, painted in the manner of 18th or middle 19th century, he ought to be suspicious.

From the beginning of the 20th century, writers have discussed and decried antique fakery. Their books help today's antiques detective to be on the lookout for reproductions of the 1900's, 1930's and 1940's. By now the reproductions will have "aged," and it will be up to the antiques detective to discover the clues that will uncover their real ages. The most interesting thing about those old books is the "kid gloves" treatment given to fakes and fakers. Usually just a brief paragraph or two and a photo or drawing alerted the collector to the shady doings in the back rooms of some of New York and London's fanciest antique shoppes. In *Furniture Treasury*, considered in 1933 the bible for collectors of antiques, author Wallace Nutting discussed reproductions. "The universe is designed for straight people. Crooks thrive only where there are many straight people to cheat." With every other person collecting antiques without knowing what he is doing, "there are many straight people to cheat."

Many collectors from time to time suffer from the "glazed eyeball syndrome." It usually happens when he or she is suddenly confronted with a plethora of antiques. Table upon table heaped high with silver, glass, and porcelain can unhinge the strongest mind. Rooms that bulge with exquisite Duncan Phyffe pieces, Chippendale candlestands, and Windsor chairs can bring on an attack of GES. The symptoms are rapid breathing, flushed face and an almost zombie-like trance that keeps the victim from making any

Even though the hardware on antique furniture may not be the original, it's a good idea to know how to date whatever hardware may be on the piece at time of discovery. It can provide a clue as to when the piece was either "updated" or restored. The brass drawer pull on the left is typical of the type used on furniture from 1830 to about 1850. The glass drawer knob was made by the Boston & Sandwich Company and was found on a large secretary-desk. The brass handle, far right, was used from about 1890 to 1905 and the design shows the influence of the Art Nouveau period. The backplate is cast brass with the bails of brass-plated iron and was used to gussy-up a country kitchen table with one drawer.

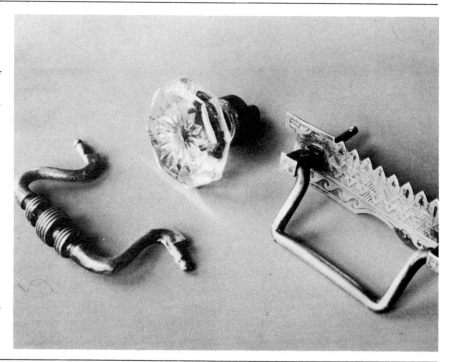

coherent plans. In its next stage of the syndrome, the victim rushes blindly forward, not stopping to add and subtract clues, grabbing without discrimination anything and everything. In this frenzy, everything looks like a rare antique. Only when it is too late and the victim sits exhausted before his "overkill" purchases, does reason return. Many antiques detectives confess to having been afflicted at least once by GES. Now when facing such overwhelming treasures, they let others rush forward. "Buy in haste, repent at

Long forgotten artists and paintings offer the antiques detective an opportunity to find something others have missed at places like church rummage sales. This old chromo-lithograph was derived from a famous painting by artist J. C. Maggs (1819-1896), considered one of the most successful painters of English coaching scenes. Queen Victoria was one of his patrons. Complete with frame, this print was a five-dollar discovery.

leisure" is their motto. The antiques detective often prefers to let the thundering herd charge past him, because in its haste it will be likely to leave choice items behind.

Patience is one of the most necessary qualities for the antiques detective. Resist the impulse that can trigger the glazed-eyeball syndrome and lead to some trashy buys. Rushing in wildly allows no time for studying marks or for looking behind doors, on top of cupboards, and under washtubs. So what if nothing was left behind? There's always another antique sale, and another, and another.

2.
The Case
of the
Missing Crown

There is nothing more deceptive than an obvious fact.
—SHERLOCK HOLMES,
in *The Adventures of Sherlock Holmes*

There is great satisfaction in purchasing a fine antique that has been rejected by over nine hundred antique dealers, collectors and browsers. By every law of averages it couldn't happen. Yet, the proof is there, softly shining with the patina of two hundred years: the American Hepplewhite chest-on-chest that I bought for one hundred fifty dollars.

The advertisement in the *Chicago Tribune* sounded very tempting. In brief, it offered a housesale with hundreds of antiques, held in an old brownstone house near the downtown area of the city. These were the furnishings and collections of the present owner, a well-traveled retired teacher in her late seventies. People were advised to bring shopping bags, for the hundreds of small *objets d'art*. The ad deftly dropped names like Chippendale and Georgian. Even on that hot July weekend a huge turnout was anticipated. The women who conducted the sale later told me that on the first day the line had gone around the block. But for some reason, I completely forgot about the sale. A phone call from two fellow collectors reminded me. They had been there on the first day and had waited two hours to get in. By the time they finally pushed through the door, there wasn't much left. Knowing I collect old bottles, they called to tell me there had been one early pressed bottle still on a shelf. But it was already two in the afternoon on the second day of the sale. By three I was rushing through the door of the old house with the last of the crowd. The large high-ceilinged Victorian rooms looked stark and badly in need of paint. Once-fine lace casements covered the windows. Only a few pieces of late-Victorian furniture remained in the living room. Two early painted tin trays and a broken chair were grabbed before I could even examine them. I first inquired about the bottle from the sellers. It had already been sold. "There isn't much good stuff left," they told me. "After all, over nine hundred people have been through here. Besides, the family lawyer had first choice. He picked out the really fine pieces of furniture; you should have seen the Chippendale chairs!" I had to admit it was not very encouraging. But perhaps the dealers had overlooked some small piece. About twenty professional dealers were still milling around, poking amid glassware, assorted pieces of silver, odds and ends. Leaving them with their dubious treasures, I began the climb to the third floor. It was like scaling Mt. Everest without help from the Sherpas. What good would it do if I did find any furniture? How could I carry it down the steep, winding stairs? Every piece remaining was tagged with a "sold" ticket. I came upon two dealers haggling over a price tag on a mahogany dressing glass with its original reverse glass painting. They couldn't decide whether to buy it and finally left it behind. It was in almost perfect condition. Picking it up, I began the trek downstairs. How often do you come across an American dressing glass, *circa* 1830, these days, at any price? After I pantingly set the piece down on the checkout table, I decided to take a closer look around on the first floor. Jokingly, one of the sales people asked, "Have you investigated the coal cellar? There's some stuff in there. All you have to do is climb up on a couple of chairs to get through the crawl space." How could I pass up such an opportunity? Disregarding my white slacks, I climbed atop two teetering pieces of furniture and into the coal bin. The ceiling was so low I had to walk almost on my knees, but I was sure that none of the dealers had been so adventurous as I. Shining my handy flashlight around, I spotted absolutely nothing. Apparently all nine hundred dealers, browsers, and collectors had crawled around the coal bin. Dusting myself off, I mumbled, "Enough is enough," and prepared to pay for the dressing glass. As is the custom, the checkout table stood wedged almost into the corner, next to the massive front door. For the first time since I had entered the house, I looked behind the table at a towering dark brown mass of wood. I did a double-take: the mass was a chest-on-chest of some sort. "Don't make out the bill just yet," I said, edging around towards the massive piece of furniture. It stood at least six feet tall. The feet splayed outward and the entire piece curved gracefully in a bow front. As neglected and in need of a good polishing as it was, the rich graining of mahogany was still obvious. The oval-shaped brasses seemed to have a design stamped on them. "Has this been sold?" I asked. Almost with indifference one of the sellers said, "No, but we're taking closed bids on it. The price is three hundred fifty dollars. The top is missing." In my excitement over the basic design of the piece, I hadn't noticed that, indeed, the "crown" was missing. But what kind of a crown had it been? "What happened to the crown?" I queried. "Why don't you ask the owner? She's right here," said the seller.

A handsome, authentic Hepplewhite chest-on-chest isn't your every day bargain discovery. Even without the narrow "crown" I was amazed that no one had bought it, even at the original asking price of three hundred fifty dollars. Except for the slight warping on the right side of the case, the piece is in good condition. As you can see, it is being used for practical storage and the chest is as useful and handsome today as it was over one hundred and fifty years ago.

The original bail handles in heavy cast brass helped me put the chest-on-chest in historical perspective. This "ear of corn" design is one of many used during the Hepplewhite period, including the American eagle and sheaf of wheat.

A spritely little woman in her late seventies had been watching me with some amusement. "You think that piece is something? Well, it isn't," she said with obvious relish. "I had some really fine things. But this piece that I bought in New Orleans only cost me a couple of hundred dollars. I bought it back in the 1930's. I remember it well, because when I was about to go into the antique shop, a parade of cars with Franklin Roosevelt in one went by and he waved at me." She didn't remember what the missing top had looked like, but she did recall vividly what became of it. "That following winter was very cold. This old house used to take a lot of coal. We had run out of all the coal and even firewood. So, my sister and I lifted the top off of that chest and threw it in the fire."

I couldn't suppress a shudder. It was sacrilege to use the top of a Hepplewhite chest-on-chest to warm your hands. By then I had realized that this was a Hepplewhite-style chest-on-chest, though at that point I wasn't sure of the exact date of the piece. Superficially it appeared to be of the actual Hepplewhite period, around 1810. The seller informed me it was probably French, since it had come from New Orleans. "Probably came in at the docks." Whatever it was, I didn't have three hundred fifty dollars to spend on it. Doubting I would ever see it again, I wrote my name and phone number along with a closed bid of one hundred fifty dollars on a small piece of paper. The fact that a very important piece, the crown, was missing and would be difficult to replace didn't really make an impression on me. I only regretted that I would probably never again have a chance to purchase such a fine piece of furniture at such a low price. A piece like that would, when fully restored, be worth from seven to nine thousand dollars, especially if it were American. But why had no one bought it for that ridiculous sum? One of the sellers suggested its size had deterred its purchase. "Not many people have rooms that will accommodate a piece like that." Nonsense! Dealers can always find some American collector who would, if necessary, stuff it into the kitchen rather than pass it up.

Almost as soon as I walked in my front door, the phone rang. The chest-on-chest was mine. When could I pick it up? Since it needed restoration, I decided to have a trusted cabinetmaker, someone who was capable of making a copy of the missing crown, give an estimate and take it directly to his workshop. The restorer I chose gave me an estimate of five hundred fifty dollars and a waiting period of several months. I assured myself that by that time, I would be able to pay him. I didn't see the chest-on-chest again till the cabinetmaker returned it to me three months later, gleaming with brass, french-polished, and topped with a proper crown aged to match the rest of the piece.

What did I see that others didn't? As an antiques detective I first saw *what it seemed to be:* a chest-on-chest made of mahogany in the style of Hepplewhite, around 1800. The bow front is formed in two segments. The top supports three full and two half-drawers. The crown is missing. The base supports three full drawers. The drawers are pine. It is mounted on two curved bracket (French style) feet and two simple rear bracket feet.

Clues and Deductions: Saw marks on the inside of drawers and on the back indicate the piece was made before the 1830's, when the circular saw came into use. The jagged marks of the pit or frame saw then in use are easy to see. However, when dating a piece like this, you have to consider where the piece was made. If it was made far from the main furniture centers of the East where the styles were set, it might have been made as late as 1830. It is not "high style," but was made by a skilled cabinetmaker. Thus, it should probably be considered a country piece. Because the drawers and secondary wood are pine, you can assume it is American.

The drawer bottom shows yellow pine graining. However, many English drawer bottoms may be made of Norway spruce or fir. Yellow pine was extensively used in early American furniture and is now almost nonexistent. It is an extremely heavy wood. Notice how the curved bow front of mahogany is dovetailed into the pine drawer. The blocks on the bottom of the drawer were another device used by the cabinetmaker to help the bottom of the drawer glide smoothly without sticking. The marks of the early saw are also visible.

This detail of side of the drawer shows the rough marks of the old plane and a single pine knot. These joiner marks usually show up on the underside of drawers and the backs of chests. To the right of the dovetails, you can see the score marks. The cabinetmaker used them as a guide to line up the dovetails.

Replacing a missing part takes time and further research. In this instance, I went through books on the Hepplewhite style. The final result was a simple ogee moulding. If I hadn't told you, you'd never know it was brand new, unless you were an antiques detective.

When you look back, it seems elementary. When you take the piece apart the details or clues all fall into place. What if I had been influenced by the sellers who had had the house and contents appraised by experts? Or what if I had been put off by that fact that close to a thousand buyers had rejected the chest-on-chest? In the world of antiques nothing is elementary.

Let's assume that the piece had been made in the 20th century with "intent to deceive." The back of the chest-on-chest would have been of smooth wood and not in the wide, uneven widths of rough board. An antiques detective can often make an instant deduction, without even *looking*, simply by running a hand across the back of the piece.

The brasses on the new piece would have numbers on the inside and possibly be made of iron covered with brass. Testing with a magnet would de-

The presence of old nails may or may not be indicative of authenticity. This nail, removed from the back of the drawer, has a hand-forged head and shank, in keeping with the appropriate historical period.

termine this. Nails might not be old ones; much depends on the degree of fakery involved. The dovetailing on the drawer would be uniform, machine-made. Bottoms of the drawers would be smooth. However, a clever dealer might explain away these discrepancies by saying that since the piece was so old, the drawers had had to be restored. The back of the piece as well as insides of drawers might have factory-made numbers printed on them. When examined from the inside, without the drawers, a new piece would be smoothly planed. And in the case of the chest-on-chest, the top of the lower chest would be covered with board. In a genuinely old piece, the lower chest wouldn't have a top.

Family histories of pieces may be either helpful or confusing. There was only one clue in the seller's tale: the fact that she paid only a couple of hundred dollars in the 1930's for it. At that time, authentic Hepplewhite pieces weren't popular and could have been purchased for a low price, as could Sheraton pieces, which are only now reaching any kind of price peak.

An obviously hand-forged steel lock on the drawer provides another clue to its age. Notice the irregularity of the holes and the hammer marks, slightly curved lines on the left side, near the holes.

An old steel key, probably not the original, is also hand-forged.

3.
The Story
Behind the Story

Just as in the newspapers, the story behind the headlines is often more exciting. This is particularly true when the subject involves antiques. Unless an antique comes with a pedigree, most collectors will never know the history of their possessions. That is why it's always more fun to own a chamberpot you know belonged to somebody famous, a bed that George Washington supposedly slept in, or the first typewriter ever used by Ernest Hemingway. It's a part of that good old antique mystique. There are, of course, outrageous stories concocted by dealers and sellers alike, surpassing Scheherazade's "A Thousand and One Nights." I guess I'm lucky I write an antiques column that has an alert readership. Whenever I have an object I'd like to learn more about, I take a picture of it, research it as far as I can, and share it with my readers. There's a good chance that I'll hear from someone with first-hand information or from some reader who has an object like the one I've written about and who wants to sell it to me. Such unlikely items as a bookplate, a trophy, and a furniture label are among the objects with behind-the-scenes stories.

Crossing the Mississippi on a raft may have been fine for Huck Finn, but at my advanced years, it's something I could have done without. Yet, as an antiques detective I had to follow down an exciting lead, regardless of where it led. A column on old pie safes resulted in a letter from Mr. F., who wrote that he had three of them in his basement and would be glad to sell them to me cheap, just to get rid of them. It's not every day that a city girl runs into one of the mid-19th-century cabinets with punched tin doors. As their name suggests, they were used to store freshly made pies. The choicest safes have ornate designs of stars, hearts, and scrolls punched into tin doors and panels. From Mr. F.'s description his safes were really choice. In the city these might cost upwards of three hundred dollars when refinished. Of walnut, pine or poplar, the cabinets stand on straight, tall legs, out of reach of mice. Mr. F. lived somewhere in Illinois, near the Mississippi River. I found his town on the map, with an indicated population of over two hundred souls. Mr. F. had also written that he was cleaning out his old barn and might find some other antiques for me. I could hardly wait, and it looked simple enough to get to his place. I just needed to take the tollways to the proper turnoffs and towns. I decided to make the trip during the time my husband was on a business trip in nearby St. Louis. I set off confidently with a neighbor and one son for company. Asking directions in every neighboring town on the map, we followed a bumpy, winding road that curved around hills that seemed more like mountains. There were no street names or numbers on the few houses scattered about; in fact, you couldn't even say there was a street. Calling out to a farmer walking down the road, I asked if he knew Mr. F. "You're in front of his house," he told me. After I drove up another hill, Mr. F. and his wife greeted me. Taking me into his neat basement, he showed me not only the three pie safes but a pine jelly cabinet with original paint, several pressed-back chairs and an old carbon auto lamp. "Thought you might like this lamp. It come from an old Maxwell. A feller offered me thirty dollars, but I saved it for you." All of us eagerly loaded one pie safe inside the station wagon, the jelly cupboard on top, and the auto lamp in the front seat. I was willing to put another pie safe atop the cupboard. "Wouldn't do that if I wuz you," cautioned Mr. F. "It might be too heavy a load for the barge." In unison, we chorused, "What barge?"

"Why, the one that will take you over to St. Louis. You just honk the horn at the river bank and they come over to git you. Otherwise, you have to take some out-of-the-way back roads to go to St. Louis. That would take you three hours. The barge will take you only about five minutes."

With Mr. F. leading the way in his pickup truck, our overloaded station wagon headed towards the Mississippi. Sure enough, we honked and what looked like an oversized raft headed towards our side of the shore. The trip cost two dollars, one way. As the car was chained to the raft, I noted uneasily the warning sign, "Not responsible for accidents." Now, looking back at the excursion, it was fun. But who will believe me when I tell them that I, my pie safe and jelly cupboard crossed the Mississippi on a raft?

The story of the silver queen began in a small mining town in Utah, and ended in a Chicago suburb, the journey made by a small paper bookplate, pasted inside a volume of Henry Thoreau's *Cape Cod,* and bearing the name, Susanna B. Holmes.

For a long time I had been intrigued by the variety of designs used on bookplates. While there are still collectors of bookplates, today's younger generations generally don't even know what one is. Yet for several centuries, the proud owner of fine volumes personalized them with a small piece of pa-

A detail of the Susanna B. Holmes' bookplate shows an Art Nouveau design. The designs of bookplates followed the popular art of their times. If this were of the Hepplewhite or Sheraton period, it would probably have the popular scallop-shells or ornamental designs of that time. The Holmes' bookplate recalls the days when large home libraries were in fashion and the books in them were actually read and displayed by wealthy collectors. Many antiques detectives look only for books that can't be repaired, in order to salvage the bookplates. Some bookplate collectors would use the Holmes' bookplate as part of a specialized collection, to focus on either women collectors or the artist, C. C. Snow. Many well-known artists designed bookplates, among them, Walter Crane and Kate Greenaway.

per, bearing a design or picture with his or her name. Needing a bookplate to photograph for my column, I chose one at random from my shelves. It displayed two Art Nouveau figures and the name, Susanna B. Holmes. I knew only that it was part of a collection of books that had come from my late uncle's home in Pasadena, California, after his death and that he had acquired his library at book auctions during the 1930's and 1940's.

Shortly after the bookplate column appeared, I received a letter from James Darling, of San Diego, asking how I came into possession of a Susanna Holmes' bookplate. He wrote that one rainy night in 1937 he and several hundred other antique book collectors and dealers had attended a rare book auction, in the Pasadena, California, mansion of the late Susanna Holmes. In the great American tradition, Susanna's first husband, a poor

You may not want to collect old trophies like this one, but presentation pieces are almost in the same category. Perhaps you'll encounter some silver loving cups or trays with interesting histories. Historical significance counts most with collectors of presentation pieces. A silver bowl presented to Mrs. Abraham Lincoln on her wedding anniversary (if such a thing should exist) is an example. Less glamorous, but still collectible would be the trowels used by various city mayors to lay the cornerstones of public buildings.

prospector in Utah, finally struck pay dirt with his silver mine. Susanna became known as "The Silver Queen," after her husband's mine, The Silver Queen. Her husband died six years later, leaving her rich, young, and beautiful, like the heroine of the old soap opera, "Our Gal Sunday." As she married and remarried over the years, she became Susanna Bransford Emory Holmes Delitch Engaliticheff. She indulged herself by purchasing beautiful rare antiques, especially books. Some of the books weren't that rare. At the auction they were sold by the stack for as little as two and a half dollars. It was quite a sale, at least for Mr. Darling. "The sale ran from 7:30 P.M. to 3:45 A.M. and attracted every book dealer in southern California. It was the high point of my many years of auction going," he wrote.

Yesterday's winner began as a humorous antiques column, based on the so-called shortage of inexpensive antiques and collectibles. While wandering through a Chicago suburb, I paused to look in a jewelry store window at a push-up brass candlestick. Beside it stood a silver boxing trophy, the figure of a young man in boxing shorts, ready to throw a punch at an invisible opponent. The date engraved on the base was 1932. While so far I hadn't come across any collectors of old trophies, a column on the subject might open up an entire new collecting field.

The trophy was inscribed to Gene Higgins and was decorated with two crossed flags, Italian and American. I took the trophy home and wrote a tongue-in-cheek column about trophy collecting. Meanwhile, I had the old-timers on the newspaper sports desk check back files for mention of Gene Higgins or of the match he had won, but they found nothing. Then, to my amazement, after the column appeared, I received a letter from Higgins' cousin. She wrote that he had been a lightweight champion boxer in the Catholic Youth Organization in the Chicago area. Boxers came from Italy to compete and Gene won the trophy. Higgins had died six years before and the trophy had somehow found its way to the small jewelry shop. "From now on I'm going to pay closer attention when browsing in antique shops—everything must have a history," his cousin noted.

A royal tale from Honolulu is a favorite story of mine. On one of my visits to the Iolani Palace in Honolulu I asked curator James Bartells if he ever found any royal antiques at garage sales. Has he ever! Before there was any thought to restoring the Palace, its furnishings were sold at auction. Today they could be anywhere in the world. A great hunt has been going on for years for the original royal furnishings that had belonged to King Kalakaua. From some photographs and descriptions, Bartells had an idea of what was missing and what it looked like. Like most museum curators, he gets calls regularly from people who are sure they have some of the missing objects. Fortunately, some of them really do. On one particularly humid day, Bartells got a call from a man who was certain he had one of the chairs from the throne room. Bartells immediately drove to the caller's home. Although that particular chair didn't fit the description, as he was leaving, Bartells looked through an open garage door to see, partially covered with old rags and oozing stuffing, one of the actual throne room chairs. The owner couldn't believe the battered old chair that the dog had chewed up had once belonged to King Kalakaua. Another time Bartells spotted a throne room chair in a Honolulu Salvation Army Thrift Shop. As an antiques detective, he has implanted the pictures of those chairs and other furnishings in his mind's eye, and sooner or later he believes he'll have the complete set back in the Palace.

The mysterious label was a great challenge to me for a long time. As I look at it now, everything seems so obvious that I think I must have been suffering from the glazed eyeball syndrome at the time I purchased my labeled game table. An antiques detective doesn't usually go out looking for a specific antique and expect to find it at a house sale unless it is advertised as part of the furnishings. Since so many antiques are mislabeled and poorly described, the antiques detective comes to be suspicious of all labels, descrip-

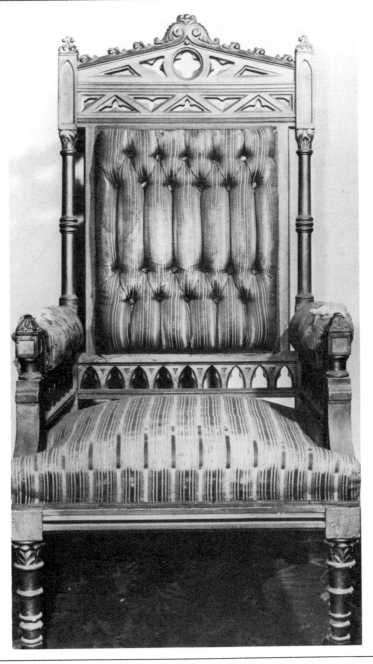

Have you seen any throne room chairs like this one? Made in Boston in 1882 by A. H. Davenport & Company for Hawaiian King Kalakaua, it was found in a garage by an antiques detective. The entire wood surface is gilded. The original upholstery was crimson silk damask.

tions, and sales tags. There is no way of knowing what will actually be at a house sale. Nevertheless, as I waited my turn on the apartment stairs to view the advertised "antique game table," I was hoping it was a Sheraton. These are the favorites of every antique show. Their prices range from a thousand to two thousand dollars. Even if the house sale price were four hundred dollars such a table would still be a find and fifty dollars would be more my speed. By listening to the shop talk of the dealers ahead of me, I learned the estate belonged to a once wealthy, middle-aged woman, now an alcoholic. As a matter of fact, she was snoring in a drunken stupor behind a closed bedroom door while the sale went on. According to rumor, most of the pieces were choice antiques from New England. But isn't every antique with a bit of class some legendary New England piece? As I listened, I craned my neck to see who the dealers were. I recognized them mostly as buyers of silver, rugs and glass, but not of furniture. I stood a fighting chance to acquire the table.

It was easy to spot. I gave it a quick psyching-out as the crowd shoved and pushed into the room. Outwardly it looked right. The serpentine top, bordered with banding, and the inlaid fruitwood medallions were clues by which to identify a typical Sheraton game table. Similar pieces had been pictured in Sotheby Parke Bernet catalogs with estimated values of from twenty-five hundred to thirty-five hundred dollars. Except for one loose leg, this one was in mint condition. It would be a prize for any furniture collector. In fact, if I hadn't been suffering from glazed eyeball syndrome, I would have realized that it looked too good. As I contemplated its purchase price of one hundred seventy-five dollars, I heard a dealer say, "Did you see that old pine dropleaf table over there with the five hundred dollar price tag?" My ears pricked. "That's an old family piece," one of the sellers noted. "Over two hundred years old. A dealer recognized it right away." I had to take a close look at this antique wonder. As I moved towards it, I breathed a sigh of relief. I wouldn't be tempted to hock the family jewels for this piece, not when it was covered by that icky orange shellac finish favored by fakers in the 1930's and 1940's. To reinforce my deductions, I borrowed a flashlight and crawled underneath. "Oh, you don't need to worry about whether it's the real thing," one of the sellers called down to me. "We've had experts tell us all about that table." At that point, a hefty dealer slapped the table top possessively and informed us, "I'm buying that. You don't need to bother looking at it anymore."

I didn't need to look at it anymore. By that time I had discovered the hinges were all brand new, as were nails and screws. But the lack of telltale tool marks and the too-perfectly matched legs, showing no wear at the feet, clinched it. To have been made in the 18th century, the table should have shown at least a handwrought nail or two. Delighted to see an expert taken in, I said nothing. Several months later at a very fancy antique show press review, I saw the same table now wearing a tag of seven thousand dollars. Much to my delight, an irate browser was roaring at the dealer, "How can you have the nerve to put a price of seven thousand dollars on a table that isn't even a good fake?" A crowd gathered as he pointed out the very clues I had noted. I am sorry to say that two ushers led him away, while the dealer muttered, "Too much to drink, poor fellow."

Meanwhile, back at the apartment sale, I took a closer look at the Sheraton game table. Pulling it out from the wall I looked at the back. A label said it had been made by Charak Furniture Company, in Boston. The lettering on the label was in the Old English style—"Bofton." Hurriedly, I paid for it and with help got it down the stairs and into my car.

When I got it home, I began to go over it for clues of age. It should have been rough and a little warped on the bottom. It wasn't. The hardware should have been old and at least one of the nails handwrought. They weren't. Yet, it was a beautiful, handmade piece. Suddenly, it was as though I were reading the label for the first time. The words "hand made" stood out in three flashing dimensions. The faker had goofed and so had I. In the 1810's and 1820's when this table supposedly was made, *all* furniture was handmade. There was no need to say so. It was totally out of historical context. I dashed to the library, still hoping that I was wrong and that the name Charak would be listed under American cabinetmakers. It was a fruitless search. But when had the piece been made? After all, hadn't it been a family heirloom, along with the gateleg table? Logic told me it must be a Centennial piece, made around 1876. It could still be an heirloom couldn't it?

This looks like an authentic Sheraton-style or Federal period card table. Notice the reeded, tapering legs, topped with ring-turned dies. A hinged serpentine top is trimmed with patterned banding. The skirt has medallions of contrasting woods.

So, I lovingly polished it and placing it in the dining room, forgot about it.

Every story has an ending, including that of my game table tale. Nearly a year later, while visiting a local Indian artifacts museum, I spotted *my* game table in the lobby. It belonged to the museum owner, who also collected antiques. He didn't mind if I moved the table away from the wall to look at the back. Sure enough, there was the same label. Where mine had a white, painted-out spot, his said, "1932." "What do you know," he chuckled, "my wife bought that as an antique years ago. We never did look at the back too carefully."

The two-dollar winner is really three tales in one, about three overstuffed old houses. Just by chance, I dropped into a hole-in-the-wall antique shop in search of photo props for my column. "You want lots of stuff to photograph, then you come to this house on Wimple Street Saturday morning," said Millie, the shop owner. "You won't believe this house. It's taken us three months just to go through enough things to price them. There's no order to the sale. You have to go through the stuff yourself. We are hoping to sell off enough privately to dealers and friends so we don't have to run an ad. There isn't any room to move around." Who could resist an invitation like that? Saturday I arrived in front of a house so full inside that many of the items had to be placed outside, protected by heavy plastic sheets. Dashing through the front door, I entered a large room with wall-to-wall tables and over-

From the back, it doesn't look quite right. Especially the aged label with its "olde" English printing.

flowing boxes. There were beer steins, Depression glass, silver, books, and furniture jammed together. Where should I begin? What should I look for? I almost lost my cool. "Just plow right in," Millie said. "There's more in the garage. And two more houses to go—just like this one."

As the hours passed, I sifted through the items, looking for objects either for my collections or for photo props. I never got past the first floor, perhaps for the best. The stairs leading to the second floor had no railing and were stacked with magazines and paintings. "The owners were amateur artists," Millie told me. "We've got so many art supplies and prints and paintings we're going to hold a separate art sale in one of the other houses." It seemed that one of the former owners, now deceased, had been a successful writer and the other, also deceased, an artist. Widely traveled, they picked up some rare artifacts, earmarked for local museums. But apparently they just kept acquiring objects and didn't know when to stop.

Stumbling through the dining room into the small kitchen, I looked around for something that would stand apart from the thousands of items. When I glanced upwards at the kitchen cabinets, I saw the warped shape of a treenware bowl, or at least that is what it looked like. Covered with dust and kitchen grease, it certainly didn't look like a fine American primitive wooden bowl. Millie said it was mine for two dollars, but wouldn't I rather have some of the good stuff like the Depression glass? As I continued picking around the boxes, I came up with an early heart-shaped trivet. Another two dollars. It was beginning to seem as if everything I selected cost two dollars. Then I spotted the Oriental rug. "We had that priced at five hundred dollars but the dealers didn't want it because it wasn't signed and is a bit worn." The rug, fourteen by fifteen feet, had an avocado ground and a colorful medallion and would be just right for my long bare dining room floor. "You can have it for a hundred and twenty-five," said Millie. Good, bad, or otherwise, what kind of a rug of any age can you buy for that price these days? For years I had been passing up Oriental rugs at house sales, not that there are many left after the dealers storm through. Somehow, too, I felt that I wouldn't know enough and would buy a poor quality Oriental. Recently there have been so many informative books on the subject, I had decided to make a study of Oriental rugs. Now the moment of truth had arrived. Did I dare to buy an Oriental that the experts had turned down? "They thought it was probably a Sarouk," Millie noted. My scant knowledge told me it wasn't a Sarouk, but a wool Tabriz. "Be sure to come to the other sales," Millie said, helping me load my purchases into the car.

One of the other houses was practically empty. But house number three was a beauty, if you assume that "beauty is in the eye of the beholder." It had apparently been used as an art supply store and to raise or board cats. I followed Millie's advice and avoided the basement. Lots of cats had once lived in dark, dank basement cages. Finding nothing in the house of interest, I went out to the garage. My eyes made out several poles with knobs on them, towering over the piles of boxes. Because of the clutter, I couldn't get any closer than six feet. They seemed to be parts of a large rope bed. I ran back into the house to see if Millie's helpers could move aside some of the trash. They could and did and sure enough, parts of an oak rope bed, crudely turned, emerged. "You can have it all for twenty-five dollars," Millie said. I looked at first one piece and then another, trying to figure out how it fit together. I finally realized that there were two head and foot boards, but unfortunately no legs. Sadly, I left it there.

Several weeks later I stopped in at Millie's shop. "You know, I think I'm going out of the antique business. Those three houses did me in. We finally had to call the junk man in to haul it all away as rubbish. Tell you what though, you can have these two old doll buggies free for your photos." Millie is all heart. The buggies, like most of the contents of the three houses, are missing a few small pieces—like wheels and tops. Shuddering, I realize that if I'm not careful, soon my house will look like Millie's last housesale.

Mr. Swensen's treasures will probably never been seen by antique collectors. Swensen is the elderly man who repairs my small antiques at phenomenally low prices and with great skill. For at least ten years I and other collectors have been taking damaged antiques to his backstreet workshop. He insists that what he repairs has at least to look like an antique. This fussiness comes from years of working as a furniture repairer and restorer in a hoity-toity antique shop. Quite frequently he mentions an older brother who supposedly works with him. "I don't know if I can fix that table, my brother isn't well and he is the one who would know how to make another leg like that one." Swensen's prices are so reasonable that all of his customers are concerned about his health as well as that of his nebulous brother. "Get that chair over to Swensen before he croaks," suggested one concerned customer. You'd be concerned, too, if you had a repair man who charged from only five to thirty-five dollars to repair legs, drawers and other antique ailments. And he always apologizes for charging so much. One day he asked me if I knew anyone who might be interested in buying some of his antiques. He and his wife wanted to clean out the garage. The poor old codger, what could he hope to make from some pitiful odds and ends? "I know you write about antiques, Mrs. Gilbert, so you will give me a fair estimate of what some of the things are worth." That put me on the spot. Even if he did have anything valuable, who could even think of cheating such a trusting old fellow? I resolved to give him my honest opinion, regardless of how tempting it might be to try to make a cheap buy. After all, I wasn't a dealer, only a collector, and I could afford to be honest. Almost patronizingly, I agreed to look over his things. It had never occurred to me, as an antiques detective, to snoop around Swensen's workshop. At first glance nothing seemed very exciting. There was a silver-plated hollow ware dish, a driftwood lamp and a large wooden carving.

"I've had this old piece since I left the other shop," he said, turning on another light. That was in the Depression, you know, and they didn't have the money to pay me. I took lots of antiques instead of money." The carving was about three feet high, of a knight in armor, holding his sword in front of him. "The man who owned this told me it was from a French ship, World

For some reason, this old carving was unappreciated by a number of collectors of nautical antiques. They might not have expected to find a two-hundred-year-old ship's ornament in the modest workshop of an elderly cabinet-maker in the Midwest. The fact that it is made of white oak, according to some wood experts, suggests the piece is American. The knight supports a curved beam. The marks of an early knife blade can easily be seen on the knees and shoulders. Hand-wrought iron nails jut out in several places, as if the piece had been wrenched free by force. It waits in Mr. Swensen's work-shop for some antiques detective to recognize the clues to its age and origin.

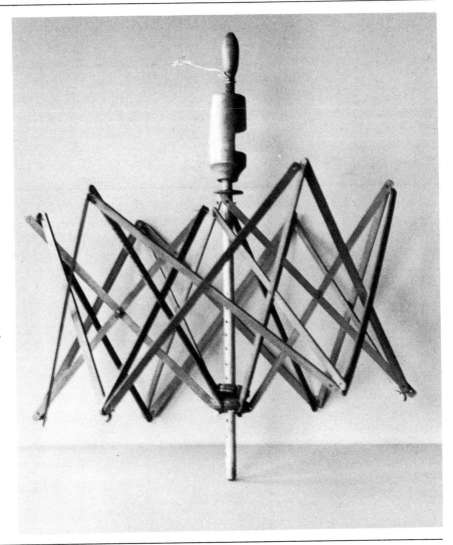

This beautifully grained maple swift would delight any textile collector. It was probably originally attached to a work table and the yarn was wrapped around it, ready for spinning. When not in use, it collapses. You don't run into these every day, especially not priced for a couple of dollars—and Mr. Swensen was delighted to get rid of it!

War I." Before I had time to take a closer look, he had snapped off the light and was pulling me towards his adjoining garage. "I want you to see this Chinese chair," he said. Bit by bit, he brought his dusty treasures into the light. Chairs, picture frames, two oil paintings someone had used as dart boards, assorted moose heads, and a maple swift were among the objects. Swensen told me the Chinese chair had to be very old and worth thousands of dollars. I saw that it was made of teak. It probably dated from around the 1870's, imported for the Philadelphia Centennial. It was a unique example. A mythological winged creature formed the back and arms and the seat was circular. Although the chair wasn't worth thousands, it would certainly bring about five hundred to seven hundred dollars in a shop. Unfortunately, like everything else he showed me, it needed repairs. Swensen was so busy repairing everybody else's antiques that he neglected his own. Examining an Art Nouveau vase filled with plastic flowers, I asked him what he wanted for

Even a torn-out single scrapbook page can be a real find. This particular page offers a variety of charming advertising trade cards from the Victorian era and is worth well over its dollar asking price in Mr. Swensen's shop.

it. "I don't think I'll sell it," he said. Trying again, I asked what he wanted for a King Kong plaster bank, probably a carnival prize. "What would you give me for it?" he asked. It was only worth about three dollars. "Well, if that is all, I might as well keep it," he said, putting it back on the dusty shelf. The cat-and-mouse game had begun. Every time I spotted some inexpensive item that would have made a good photo prop, Mr. Swensen decided he couldn't bear to part with it.

Even though I wasn't interested in the ship's carving, I felt it was a rare piece and should make Mr. Swensen a tidy profit. "Tell you what," I said. "If you load the carving into my car, I'll show it to two collectors who specialize in this type of thing. Would nine hundred dolllars be enough for it?" He became very evasive and no price was really agreed upon.

Without examining the sawmarks on the wood, the first collector proclaimed the piece a fake, probably made in Spain. He wouldn't buy it at any cost. The second expert wasn't even sure if it was a ship's carving. Whatever it was, it wasn't for him. The third expert was a dealer who sells only ships' carvings and maritime pieces. Well aware that he could sell it to a collector for twice as much as he would pay for it, I was unprepared for his response. "Well, it's interesting, but not exactly my kind of thing." He was simply unwilling to put out fair cash even for this unique carving.

The figure is back in Mr. Swensen's workshop. By now he is convinced it is priceless and wouldn't sell it, except to a museum. And his wife's third cousin's husband wants the Chinese chair for his fishing cottage. The only things Mr. Swensen would actually part with were the maple swift and a hand-carved pointing finger sign, each for two dollars. "I wouldn't feel right taking more for these old things," he said. I have since heard of several people who have lugged the ship's carving around to dealers and collectors, trying to help "the poor old fellow out." If you are ever in my neighborhood, try your gamesmanship with Swensen. You may end up with a hand-carved ship's ornament or with a headache.

4.
Confessions of Some Antiques Detectives

It is of the highest importance in the art of detection to be able to recognize out of a number of facts which are incidental and which are vital.

—SHERLOCK HOLMES,
in *The Adventure of the Reigate Squire*

How can you be an antiques detective if you don't fearlessly explore every possibility in your search for elusive objects? Sometimes they pop up in front of your eyes when you aren't even looking. Some dedicated antiques detectives are about to confess their detecting secrets and occasional errors. You may not always agree with their methods but you'll have to acknowledge that the results prove plenty of unrecognized antiques are just waiting for an antiques detective to add up clues to their identity.

Oscar Getz and the missing still. Oscar Getz isn't your everyday collector. As chairman of the board of Barton Brands he doesn't have to worry about buying antiques on a budget. Yet he derives great satisfaction in browsing through antique shops and book stores in search of items relating to the history of American whiskey, from Colonial days to Prohibition. He spends his spare time looking for items, from documents to bottles, to fill his Barton Museum of Whiskey History in Bardstown, Kentucky. He began collecting in 1933 while he was looking for a site to build a distillery in Kentucky and found an old book of distilling recipes for farmers. He has since discovered such items as a liquor license issued to Abraham Lincoln for the Lincoln and Berry Tavern, New Salem, Illinois, and the rarest of original letters, a patent granted to the inventor for an improvement in whiskey stills, with the signatures of James Monroe and John Quincy Adams. Such rarities would crown the collection of a less ambitious man than Oscar Getz. Through research he had learned that George Washington had owned and operated a whiskey still, built to his specifications on his plantation, after he retired

Oscar Getz, an antiques detective on the prowl for American whiskey artifacts, here proudly holds one of his finds, an original "booze" bottle in log-cabin shape.

In case you were wondering what an authentic still looks like, here is one with a pedigree. According to discoverer Oscar Getz, it originally belonged to George Washington.

from the Presidency. "The Daughters of the American Revolution took exception to my trying to link Washington with whiskey," Getz recalls. In his pursuit of clues Getz flew to Bristol, England, in search of records of R. Bush, manufacturer of the stills. Bombing raids in World War II had destroyed them. For a while it looked as though the identity and location of the still would remain a mystery. But a couple of years ago, the Department of the Interior asked Getz to come to Washington to help in the restoration of Ford's Theatre, especially the adjoining Star Saloon, where Booth had had a drink before assassinating Lincoln. While in Washington, Getz toured the Smithsonian Institution and their storage warehouses. The curator happened to point out an old still they had acquired from the I.R.S. The date on it was 1787 and the name, R. Bush, manufacturer. The curator said it had been confiscated, still operating, only a short time before. Its owners claimed to be descendants of the slaves who had worked the Washington plantation. Getz says though the still is now definitely authenticated, he would like to discover the original bill of sale. Meanwhile, he keeps thumbing through hundreds of volumes in secondhand bookstores. "If I have one word of advice for would-be antiques detectives, it is to research," he says. "You can't track something down if you don't know what to look for."

Gwen Trindl pursuing pewter. An eclectic collection of pewter ranging from early American to Art Nouveau makes the Trindl collection different from most. "I don't limit my collecting to 18th- or 19th-century anything," she admits. "I do most of my hunting at house and garage sales. Some of my most exciting finds have been early-19th-century American and English. One of my favorites is a charger presumed to be English, from the Revolutionary period. I bought it from an elderly woman who told me it had been brought by her family from England, then buried during the Revolution. Many pieces were destroyed at that time and melted down for weapons. It has no marks except for the look of age." While recognized marked pieces always bring more than pewter whose maker is unknown, Gwen won't hesitate to purchase unmarked pewter if it costs twenty-five dollars or less. "I'll take the chance."

Her collection of fifty pieces includes mostly middle-to-late-19th-century and, Gwen admits, is not considered of highest quality by purists. Housesale finds are among her best items. Pointing to a pewter (Britannia) chocolate pot made by the American, Gerhardt, she said, "Sometimes a piece of American pewter made as late as 1860 or 1870 can have considerable value if it is an unusual item. Even though this chocolate pot is considered Britannia, since there aren't many of this type around, it is worth a substantial sum."

A charger with the coveted Sanuel Danforth mark is another of her housesale discoveries. Generally, a charger is a dish that is eighteen inches in diameter. Collectors feel that anything less than eighteen inches is a dish or a platter. "Plates with marks are always the first to be bought, even if the collector isn't sure exactly what the mark is." A betrothal plate, probably English, was easy for Gwen to identify. Such a plate will have a triad of ini-

Gwen Trindl holds two pewter chargers, circa 1800, found at housesales in the Midwest. One is an English piece with the touchmark of Compton, Thomas & Townsend. The other bears the rare Danforth mark of the famed American pewterer.

tials; the top initial is the surname, the two lower letters are initials of the husband (left) and the wife (right).

Faking is rampant in the pewter field. However, in some cases fakes can be quite valuable. "Fakes are sometimes quite old, although not as old as they appear," Gwen observed. "Should you come across English pieces with the lion *passant,* leopard's head and other such designs, they are probably 18th-century fakes, trying to imitate objects from the 1300's. Of course, these fakes are now antiques in their own right and well worth adding to a collection. If the crowned letters are near the touchmarks and punched V.R., the piece may actually date from earlier than the beginning of Victoria's reign—1837."

Gwen pointed out that some touchmarks can be confusing. For instance, the X mark is usually English and accompanied with a crown, indicates a superior quality metal. But the crown and the X were copied from country to country. Some Americans pewterers are among those who used the X.

By comparing one similar piece with another, Gwen has learned what clues determine age, origin, and authenticity. "There is no way to fake true wear marks. An attempt to fake age gives itself away." She tests to identify Britannia posing as pewter. "Scratch the piece against white paper. If it has lots of lead in the alloy, it will leave a mark like a pencil mark." Another test is by weight. Britannia is sometimes heavier, since in the 19th century to add "body" to thin sheets of Britannia, it was wrapped around an iron core. There's an old saying that you can hear the "cry" or sound of pewter when

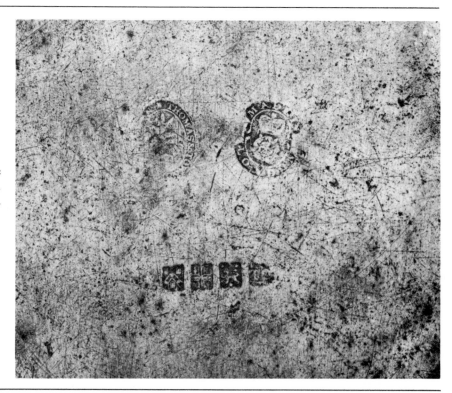

Touchmarks are still visible on this fine charger by Compton, Thomas & Townsend, London, England.

you scratch a piece then put your ear against it. But to do it correctly you have to make a deep scratch. Can you imagine a dealer letting you try that on a two-hundred-dollar piece? Concentrate on looking for other clues, like the shape and design of the pieces. Early pewter was simple in design. Later pieces attempted to copy the silver pieces of their era. The earliest plates were flat. The later large dishes had depressed centers. Since both English and American plates and chargers used rolled edges, that isn't a clue to distinguish one from the other when a piece is unmarked.

For Gwen research is essential, particularly the study of the names of the twenty-three registered Colonial craftsmen working between 1790 and 1825. "How else would I have known that Danforth was an important American name?" She points out that a large percentage of Colonial craftsmen used some form of the eagle with their name or initials as a touchmark till after the beginning of the 19th century, when the popularity of the eagle as a symbol began to wane. Pewterers began using plain initials set into an oval or square. "There are plenty of good books on the subject these days." Handles were attached after the bowl was finished. A truly antique American porringer (shallow bowl with handles used for porridges) will have a "linen" mark at the handle where the cloth-covered tongs touched the pewter. If it was made before 1807 it will have "chatter" marks, caused by the vibration of shimmying tools.

"A famous American name is important even if the piece is Britannia," Gwen advises. "The earliest Britannia designs were the same as the simple

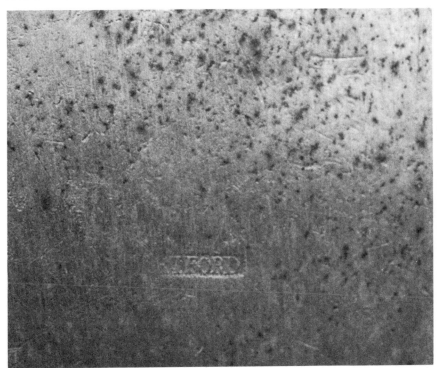

Faint, but still identifiable are the eagle and the touchmark of Samuel Danforth, American pewterer.

A genuinely historical discovery was this Indian chief souvenir painting, found by antiques detective James Williams in an antique shop, for forty-five dollars. It was painted by American artist George Cook.

pewter pieces. The Victorian age of overdesign affected Britannia like everything else. This is why some of the later pieces of Britannia are spurned by collectors.

"I also look for some of the Art Nouveau pieces made in the 1890's by Liberty Metal. It's still very inexpensive and has fascinating designs. Chinese pewter from the turn of the century up to the 1930's are budget-priced items. I don't think too many people are collecting it.

"Did you know that in the Boston archives there are records showing a shipment of pewter came to Boston from England in 1693? It consisted of several hundred pieces such as tankards, porringers, and chamber pots. Who knows when one of the pieces may turn up in someone's basement sale?" Gwen said hopefully. If that day ever comes, she'll recognize all the right clues.

James Williams' one-upmanship Americana. Williams ranks in the upper echelon of antiques detectives. Like so many others, he has discovered some of his most remarkable finds "in his own backyard," a midwestern suburb. His finds show the amazing distance antiques can travel in time and space.

As he tells it, "I was just browsing in a little antique shop when I noticed a small oil painting hanging on the wall. It appeared to be the portrait of an Indian chief. Taking a closer look, I noticed the signature, 'G.C.'" Always a collector of fine Americana, Williams admits, "At that time I wasn't too well informed about early American painters of Indian subjects. However, I assumed that the artist was George Catlin, who painted Indians in the 19th century. The price was forty-five dollars and the dealer didn't seem to know much about the painting, or it wouldn't have been priced at such a low figure. The picture wasn't really in the Catlin style, as I now know. The chief is sitting down—Catlin didn't do sitting portraits. Nevertheless, I immediately took it to the restorer to have it cleaned, which cost seventy-five dollars. When he took it apart, it appeared to have been painted on linen laminated to hard board. Even though I still wasn't sure of the painter, I did know it was an important painting. I took a slide, which I sent with a letter to the Department of Anthropology at the Smithsonian. Shortly, a letter came back from the curator. 'You don't have a Catlin but a George Cook. The painting is known as a souvenir painting. It was the custom to paint pictures of the Indian chiefs when they attended a treaty signing in Washington. Cook was a young painter attending a treaty meeting in Washington in 1825, along with a friend and fellow-artist, Charles Bird King. This painting is a portrait of Chief Coosa Tustennuggee and since it is a smaller painting, it was probably given to the chief to take back to camp (as a souvenir). Yours is one of the few souvenir paintings known to be in existence.'"

That forty-five dollar painting is practically priceless, both as American history and as a painting. When Williams saw it in that suburban antique shop, thousands of professional dealers and private collectors had passed it by. This offers a perfect example of the combination of intuition and casual knowledge resulting in a rare discovery.

Like many antiques detectives, Williams has made more than one fabulous discovery. Many antique dealers, knowing he specializes in early American antiques, contact him when they think something important has surfaced. For their services he pays them a ten percent finder's fee. "And it is well worth it." Without such help he might not have found a pair of rare inscribed James Davis brass andirons in a shop specializing in Victorian antiques. The price was two hundred seventy-five dollars and most reasonable for what they seemed to be, of 18th century origin. Supposedly they had once been owned by Artemus Ward, an American living during the Revolutionary period.

James Williams proudly examines the inscription of American James Davis on his rare brass andirons. A careful cleanup revealed the signature on the base.

Would you have recognized this as a Queen Anne chair when it had a velvet seat and Victorian grain paint? Williams saw through the disguise and deduced that the chairs were older by one hundred years than they had first appeared.

"The clue to their American origin was the steeple top, an American design. They were cast, then welded together, typical of the way they were made in the 18th century. As I looked closer, there seemed to be some kind of inscription on the base. The brass was extremely corroded where the inscription was and the problem was to clean the piece without removing the clues. Very carefully I brushed on a liquid rust remover. Then I let the piece sit for four days. When I wiped it off, the inscription, "James Davis, Boston," appeared. It's rare indeed to find a pair of brass andirons definitely ascribed to an American maker. They didn't usually sign them at all. My andirons are now valued at three and a half thousand dollars."

Detective Williams emphasizes the importance of care, when restoring any antique, and plenty of patience. Pointing out two Queen Anne side chairs with Spanish feet and a beautiful patina, he told me how careful restoration raised their value from three hundred dollars a pair to four thousand dollars.

"When I first saw these chairs in an antique shop, they had velvet seats and wood-grain painting covering their natural wood surfaces. Knowing that the velvet seats and the technique of painted wood graining were typically Victorian and thus "out of period" for chairs with Queen Anne features, I suspected that the original finish might be rescued. The trick was to remove the top layer without injuring the original finish. The average dealer would strip the whole thing and start all over, thereby lowering the value of the chairs by hundreds of dollars. I used a chemical mixture, similar to the one used for cleaning oil paintings, and when I carefully brushed it on the furniture, the original wood grain appeared. Today the chairs in their original finish are worth four thousand dollars for the pair."

Williams, like many antiques detectives (myself included), agrees that it is possible to live with an antique for years before discovering what it really is. Thirty years ago he paid a dollar and a quarter in a secondhand store in Chicago for what seemed to be an old compass. Over the years he showed it to several high school physics teachers, but they had no idea of its origin. The only clue was the name, "Thomas Greenough," on the instrument. After another ten years had passed, he wrote to the Boston Museum of Fine Arts. They identified Greenough as a mathematical instrument maker active in Boston before the Revolution. Finally, a letter from Old Sturbridge Village revealed that a Thomas Greenough "surveyor's instrument" was very rare and "very desirable." Only six had been known to exist before this: one descended through and owned by the Greenough family; one in the Franklin Institute; one at Old Sturbridge Village; the rest in other historical collections. Recently an eighth Greenough instrument turned up in Chicago at an exhibit of "The World of Jefferson and Franklin" at the Chicago Art Institute. It was on loan from the Adler Planetarium.

Williams admits that his knowledge didn't just happen. "It comes over the years by touching, feeling, and reading about the antique objects you are interested in." To get the feeling, he advises you to restore the pieces yourself when it's necessary.

"When you take something apart and put it together again, you see the marks of the original craftsman and that stays in your mind. Then when you see and touch similar objects, you'll know right away if they are genuine."

Malcom Dunn cruising for Hudson River paintings. Matter-of-factly, Dunn says, "It's a good idea to begin collecting something nobody else seems interested in." With that philosophy in mind, Dunn has acquired his own mini-museum of valuable Hudson River School paintings. As he casually admits, "If any one of them were auctioned off at Sotheby Parke Bernet these days it would be worth several thousand dollars." Even these days he avoids paying over seven and a half dollars for a painting. He is the first to tell you he couldn't afford to buy them at their appraised price. And even if he could, he probably wouldn't. For him, like most antiques detectives, the excitement comes in the process of discovery rather than in acquisition alone.

Malcom Dunn points out some of the characteristics that enabled him to find this Hudson River School painting that others had passed up. Important clues were the gauzy fabric and myriad sailboats.

His collection began about 1957 when he answered an advertisement in a Lebanon, Pennsylvania, newspaper. "There was no photograph of the painting, just the measurements and a description. The subject was a river with boats and mountains. But best of all, the price was seven and a half dollars." At that time Dunn was a young curator on the staff of Colonial Williamsburg. Like most people in the 1950's, Dunn wasn't aware of what was or wasn't a Hudson River painting or even that he should be aware. "When the painting arrived, I took it to my boss, John Merideth Graham II, who said, "That looks like a Thomas Chambers." Chambers was one of the foremost painters of the style known as the Hudson River School. Like most paintings of this type, Dunn's find was unsigned. It is now "attributed to Chambers."

Aside from Chambers and other artists known to have done this type of work, Hudson River School painting was often done by schoolgirls. It is sometimes referred to as "window shade" painting, because the gauzy fabric of which 19th-century window sashes were made was the surface for these paintings. Just what makes these amateurish paintings worth so much these days?

Reflecting, Dunn said, "Probably because they are stylized and were done in America during the period of 1825 to 1870. It really did begin with painters who lived in the Hudson River area and reflects the lifestyle of those times. People didn't travel as much in those days. And many had relatives and friends still in other countries. So it became the 'thing to do' to send these scenes to show how the Hudson River area looked."

Dunn traces the beginning of a price rise in the paintings to the 1969 first exhibit of Hudson River paintings at the Kennedy Galleries in New York. At that point they were still undervalued. These days very few turn up even at the "class" antique shows. And when they do, the prices are out of reach for the average collector.

"The Hudson River style was mass-produced near the end of the 19th century. Most of these are poor attempts to cash in on the earlier art style. Yet these days anything that even remotely resembles those early paintings is sold for top dollar."

If you want to test your luck in finding Hudson River paintings in the seven-dollar range, Dunn offers you some clues.

"Look for paintings done on a gauzy, almost translucent fabric. These are the earliest. The oils are done in a water color technique. Several color washes are put on, then the details are added. Most original early paintings have from three to seven sailboats in them. Often the sailboats are just a swipe of a brush. You'll notice the perspective isn't good in the earliest paintings. For instance, when a steamboat is in the foreground, it will be smaller than the sailboats in the background. Don't just look for sailboats. Gothic houses and ruins, as well as grotesque buildings, are also typical of the early period. These subjects were used by the painters even though they might be out of character with the rest of the painting."

Dunn believes there are still plenty of early Hudson River School paint-

A typical Hudson River School painting offered to both Americans in other sections of the country and Europeans a stylized picture of the American scene.

ings gathering dust in antique shops. "They look so amateurish, many dealers can't believe they are worth anything."

James Zipprich's silver-lined letters. "Do you know what this is?" he asked me, holding up a small silver cup on a stem. "Well, it looks like an egg cup, sort of," I suggested. "That's what many people would say. Take a closer look. It's slightly different in shape than a common egg cup. It's a goose-egg cup and worth much more than if it were an ordinary egg cup." As it turned out, the tiny cup was one of Zipprich's great discoveries. It was found in an antique shop for eleven dollars and bears the date letters of London, 1792. His knowledge of the various shapes of date letters enabled him to recognize the cup as Georgian and not Victorian. "Each 20-year cycle in silver uses a different alphabet design. I try to memorize which alphabet represents the early years. The antique dealer placed the cup in the wrong date cycle, making it 19th-century and worth only eleven dollars. There were two other clues. The cup was lathe-turned." As he held the cup towards me, I could see the telltale rings, still visible on the silver. "My research showed that lathe-turned silver was common until 1800. And the inside of the piece showed it had been gilded, also typical of the late Georgian period."

As a result of his research, antiques detectives James Zipprich recognized this goose-egg cup. Shape and size made it different from the common egg cup and much more valuable.

Zipprich admits that because silver is worth so much money today, there aren't many great finds. But he holds out hope for the dedicated antiques detective. "Fortunately, dealers don't usually mark silver things correctly. That's why I do most of my looking in antique shops. Among the easiest early silver pieces to find are spoons, which is one reason I specialize in collecting them. One of my rarest spoons was mismarked as a middle-Georgian English spoon. It turned out to be Chinese Export with false lion *passant* marks. The maker, with the initials, S.S., was an early well-known Chinese Export silversmith."

How was Zipprich able to recognize a Chinese-made spoon as such, even with its imitation English marks? He reads everything on silver that he can get his hands on and has trained his mind to retain the images he sees. He credits an article on Chinese Export silver in *Antiques* magazine for alerting him to the look and marks of such pieces.

"The spoon didn't have the appearance of an English silver spoon. For example, it had an oval bowl, thick stem, and thinner end. Georgian spoons have a more pointed bowl. It is the earliest design I've seen and it appears to be mid-18th century." He paid the standard price of fifteen dollars in the shop. Today it is worth many times that.

He began collecting silver twenty-five years ago. Unlike most collectors, he had decided what he wanted to collect and had set aside a substantial sum for his first purchase. He was prepared to pay seven hundred dollars for his first venture into silver collecting, a serving dish with a Paul Storr hallmark. Since Storr was recognized as one of the greats in English Georgian silver, he couldn't go too far wrong. Smiling like the cat that ate the canary, he says softly, "That dish is worth four thousand dollars today."

"Small items offer the collector the best opportunities," he suggests, reaching for a Georgian wine label. "Twenty years ago, when I began adding Georgian wine labels to my collection, I was able to buy a Peter and Anne Bateman label, *circa* 1794, for fifteen dollars. Now it would cost me one hundred eighty dollars. Decanter labels are a current and expensive fad."

Many collectors who are just beginning mistake scratch-mark numbers for dates. Zipprich showed me a nutmeg grater with the scratch-mark 1810. "This isn't a date. Rather, it is a pawn or repair number."

There are many problems for new collectors, according to Zipprich. "There is a lot of Hester Bateman being faked. It gets rather ridiculous at times, since many of the authentic Bateman pieces aren't worth their present price tags. Quite a few were very light and the designs weren't that good. Once you have seen a few Bateman pieces, you'll learn to recognize the decorative motifs she used. Use the old test for detecting fake hallmarks: blow on the hallmark; if it is fake, your breath will show that the mark was soldered on, not punched. Also, don't just buy a name. Names raise prices. Collectors have to pay a terrible price these days for anything by Storr, Bateman or Lamerie. It is more important that the collector make his own judgments and discover the work of a less popular, but fine silversmith. Oth-

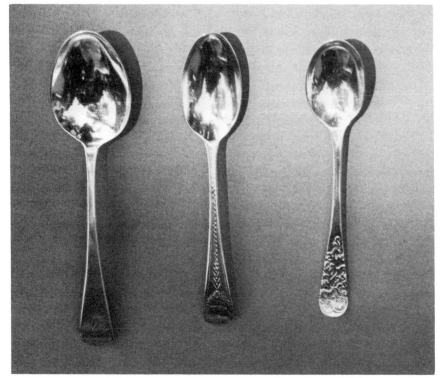

Just by looking at their shapes, James Zipprich can make a deduction as to age and origin of these spoons. Can you? One is 18th-century English, another, Chinese Export, and the third 19th-century.

Does it help to see the hallmarks and more of the design? The spoon on the left is Chinese Export, mistaken by a dealer for middle-Georgian English; the middle spoon is late-18th-century, London. The third is an early-19th-century teaspoon. The clue to the Chinese piece is in the shape of the bowl. If it were actually Georgian, the bowl would be more pointed.

erwise, he will pay through the nose."

Zipprich recalls one of his outstanding finds, a fork. "I was browsing in a shop when a man walked in off the street with a suitcase of flatware, mostly Rogers Brothers plate. However, when I took a closer look, I saw two unusual forks which, because of my research, I recognized as 18th-century French. They cost me ten dollars apiece. Because they date to the French Revolution and earlier, when so much was lost or destroyed, they are scarce. They are worth a hundred dollars each today."

He advises collectors to learn styles, decorations, and shapes common to a particular period. It is important then to distinguish between good, better, best, or bad, on the basis of appearance. "Detail work often determines value," he says. "There are always clues to help a serious collector determine date and origin of the piece. Ask yourself if the hallmarks are in the wrong place. The silversmith usually put hallmarks on after the piece was finished and decorated. In the hands of a Victorian faker a piece that may have begun as a simple piece from the Georgian period was heavily engraved in the Victorian taste. It was a common practice to heavily engrave Georgian berry spoons. This lowers their value to that of Victorian pieces."

He agrees you can't win all the time. "Once several years ago, I helped out a friend who was holding a conducted housesale of a probated estate. I discovered a Georgian solid-silver salver (a type of serving tray) made in 1738, priced at seventeen dollars. I put the correct price of fifteen hundred dollars on it and the owners decided to keep it. That was the one that got away."

Joseph Fell's Oriental rug hangup has turned pleasure into business. Ordinarily, I wouldn't include a professional dealer in my sanctified chapter on antiques detectives, but in the antique world there is always some kind of exception. Besides, he is also a bonafide antiques detective who began collecting Oriental rugs as an art form back in 1968. Other people were only putting them on the floor and more were getting rid of them in exchange for wall-to-wall plush. Fell operates his business today as part-shop, part-art gallery. Back in 1968 he was a magazine writer and antique collector. As he tells it, "One day I decided to use a check for a free-lance article to buy something really good in antiques. My wife and I went into a little shop and became fascinated with the looks of old Oriental rugs. I bought my first one from a ninety-year-old Armenian dealer. When I began to do research, I found ninety-nine per cent of the Oriental rug dealers didn't know anything about rugs. At that time there was no interest in rugs as an art form. Bit by bit, I began buying a few rugs that I had learned to identify as of high quality. By 1970 I had made up my mind that I liked rugs better than writing. I sacrificed half of my best rugs and opened my gallery. You notice I say 'gallery?' That was my new concept for selling rugs. Many previously unappreciated Orientals, such as bag faces, could now be displayed and sold as a form of art."

Fell tells about the mass shipments of hand-woven bag faces from the Caucasus and central Asia that were shipped to the United States in the ear-

The difference between antiques detective Joseph Fell and others who sell Oriental rugs is in his attitude. The finest Oriental rugs Fell discovers are hung on the wall and treated like works of art.

ly 1920's and sold at Macy's in New York for five dollars each. A bag face covered the saddle bag flung over the camel's back and gave it a little pizzazz. These nomadic pieces weren't seriously collected till forty years ago. Today you'd pay four hundred dollars for a shop's fine examples. You'd hang it on the wall like any other work of art. Fell notes that by now those 1920's bag faces are probably all over the country, turning up in house and garage sales. Whether or not you spot them depends on how good an antiques detective you are. Would you expect to find a rare bag face in an unexpected place, like draped over a rusty bird cage?

"I bought a Belouchi bag face from a dealer recently for a fraction of its value," Fell said, "for seventy-five dollars." In the collecting of rugs, he advises, "The premium is on knowledge. Talk to other collectors, read up, and look for quality of color and wool (if it is wool), as well as an interesting design. The drawing should be sharp and clear. How well a rug is woven is important. In village rugs, of course, the weave will be coarse. In city pieces, it will be more refined."

What makes two seemingly similar rugs differ widely in price? According to Fell, the combination of design and colors can separate a six-thousand-dollar rug from a fifteen-hundred-dollar rug. He advises collectors to study carefully the designs and to compare them. The eye gradually becomes trained to see the best and the worst features. Fell thinks there are still bargains to be found in shops and at private sales "if you are alert and knowledgeable." As a writer, he was accustomed to research. Thus, as a rug collector, he painstakingly studied the characteristics and designs of the different tribes who made the rugs.

He suggests that collectors on a budget might find the best buys in unrestored rugs. "The surface may be slightly thin and need tinting. A dealer wouldn't buy it because of the price of restoration. But a collector can enjoy its beauty as it is and restore it whenever he has the money."

I asked Fell about a new Oriental rug come-on, selling a piece of a rug, .like shares of stock. Some Oriental rugs ranging in value from two thousand to twenty thousand dollars are offered by a dealer as an investment. It is sold in shares and resold as often as is profitable. The buyer never actually owns the rug, may not even see it, much less wrestle with his dog on it. When the market in Orientals is up, the buyer is in luck. He can point to his bare living room floor and as in "The Emperor's New Clothes," he can ask, "How do you like my thirty-thousand-dollar Kurdish Whey? It just went up twenty points at the market today!" Fell shuddered at the thought. "This isn't collecting," he said. "I think it is pretentious of anyone to assume he has some superior knowledge as to whether the prices of Orientals will go up or down. Why own a piece of a rug when you can enjoy a beautiful rug of your own for much less than twenty thousand dollars?"

Well, it might be fun to go visit your rug on rainy days. You might meet some of your fellow investors and stand around discussing the rug market. That's got to be status, even if it isn't collecting.

The very words *Oriental rug* conjure up visions of mystic kingdoms and

Among the bargains hanging on Fell's wall are a Kaski pouch (left) purchased for one hundred seventy-five dollars and a Senneh mat, purchased from a collector for three hundred fifty dollars.

A Sorenak bag face (left) considered a find for four hundred fifty dollars and a Baluchichi bag face recently purchased from a dealer for seventy-five dollars are also part of Fell's collection. The latter has since been appraised at six hundred dollars. If you know what you are doing, you can discover valuable Orientals even in antique galleries.

flying carpets—a world as unreal as some of the current prices for Orientals. There is something positively frightening about shopping for an Oriental rug, be it in a shop or at a private sale. The antique mystique long built up around Oriental rugs can discourage even an antiques detective. The seller approaches you with, "This is a fine rug; there are so many knots to the inch." Did you ever actually try to count those knots to the square inch? Even with twenty-twenty vision and a strong magnifying glass, it's practically impossible. But do you ever ask the all-knowing, slightly mysterious, usually Armenian rug dealer how he can count them with his naked ninety-year-old eyes and you can't? Of course not. The dealer may point to some exotic Arabic figures and proclaim, "See, it is even signed and dated!" Can you read Arabic? Can the dealer? As an antiques detective you shouldn't even go near a rug dealer's digs, until you learn some of the tricks of the rug trade. Perhaps the rug with the "signature" was made the day before yesterday, or fifty years ago. The dates probably state it to be two or three hundred years old. The signature may be a humorous old Armenian proverb that translates as, "It is a wise man who is a skeptic." Rugs with such sentiments have long been found by wide-eyed travelers in Istanbul marketplaces. As they are sold and resold, the legend of the signature is told and retold. Since no one can translate, no one asks embarrassing questions and the price on a rather rotten Turkish rug continues to rise.

How can you learn about such a foreign item when even antique dealers usually don't know what they are doing? You might begin by reading every book on Oriental rugs you can get your hands on. Or you might be lucky enough to talk to an antiques detective who specializes in Oriental rugs. And he probably isn't even an Armenian!

Jane Ryden's trim-the-tree treasures were once ignored by antique dealers. Mrs. Ryden, a professional illustrator, appreciated the hand-painted quaint ornaments before others even thought about them. "Even a few years ago, I could find handblown German Christmas ornaments left over at housesales," she notes. "Today, they're one of the first things to be snapped up by dealers." Her collection of over one hundred ornaments also includes papier-mâché, paper, and carved wooden decorations. The more unusual the subject, the higher the current price. "A quaint owl, Victorian spaniel, or a Santa can be priced from ten to thirty dollars these days. Among the hardest items to find are the handblown glass chains. Apparently the tiny ball-shaped ornaments were destroyed when the string they were attached to rotted away. While the most desirable ornaments are those with their paint in good condition, no collector would pass up a unique ornament just because some of the paint had worn off. That adds to the charm." Mrs. Ryden doesn't restrict her collection to Victorian Christmas ornaments. "Highly collectible are 20th-century ornaments in Art Nouveau or Art Deco period motifs. Cars, planes, trains and boats from the early 20th century are getting scarce," Mrs. Ryden cautions. Along with ornaments, early Christmas lights, especially "bubble" lights and those with such characters as Felix The Cat, Santa, and Mickey Mouse, are worth a second glance. So far, early lights are priced as low as fifty cents a bulb, at housesales, flea markets, and antique shops. "Selectivity makes the difference between a good collection and one that is just a mishmash of ornaments." Trading with the few fellow collectors of her acquaintance has added some unusual ornaments to

The 19th-century ornaments and early handblown 20th-century ornaments, such as these, are fragile. In the front row is the German pressed paper ornament. The old car dates from around the 1920's.

her collection, at little cost. She prefers to trade rather than buy, especially since the recent number of dealer advertisements for old Christmas ornaments shows that one more antique category is on the way up in price. But that is one of the challenges that separate the antiques detective from everyone else!

5.
Understanding the Oriental Mystique

There is nothing so unnatural as the commonplace.
—SHERLOCK HOLMES,
in *The Adventures of Sherlock Holmes*

Even Charlie Chan would be perplexed by the thousands of Oriental objects sold as antiques. Astronomical prices are asked for anything Chinese and even these days "made in Japan" or "made in occupied Japan" puts a ring in the old cash register. Serious collectors of Canton (Chinese porcelain), especially blue and white, have to do some careful examining before accepting any authentication.

You don't have to settle for chop suey porcelain, hokey Satsuma and badly reproduced Japanese woodcut prints if you are willing to spend a little time studying the museum displays of fine Oriental *objets d'art* and if you notice what types of Oriental antiques are suddenly showing up in quantity at antique shows. There was lots of blue and white Canton made in the 18th and 19th centuries, but not quite as much as is for sale these days. For instance, I keep running into large numbers of covered dishes in blue and white, in very good condition, at antique shows around the country. Having seen some of the original 18th- and 19th-century ware I have *déjà-vu* working for me. The pieces I've observed in quantity at the shows are not the same blue and white. The white is greenish, the patterns blurred. All in all, it doesn't look quite right.

Jack Sewell, curator of the Oriental Arts Department of the Art Institute of Chicago agrees it is "very difficult" to provide a rule of thumb for identifying Chinese, Japanese or Korean pieces that are "terribly similar in appearance." Removing a few classic examples from the museum's displays, he carefully explained, "The trained eye of the dedicated collector can detect and understand the difference in the blues of blue and white ceramics. Basi-

Canton, Chinese blue and white, or Chinese Export, call it what you will, plates like these, once exported by the thousands to Europe and America from China beginning in the 18th century, are still being reproduced. Most of what turns up at garage and housesales was made after 1891. At that time U.S. Customs insisted on such imports being marked "China" or "made in China." Some of the paper labels eventually disintegrated. Other unmarked pieces were brought back by tourists and missionaries. Both of these plates lay claim to being Canton. One has a more blurred pattern and the white is more greenish than in the other. Both are porcelain and neither have any marks. My deductions are that both are middle-19th-century from China.

cally, the Japanese blue has a certain greyness that cannot be confused with good Ming blue. Also, the Japanese white is more a grey-green." He also explained the difference between pieces designed for "home" use and those for export. "You'll find export pieces were usually of poor quality during the Ch'ing period (1644-1908). They were heavily decorated to disguise their inferior quality." He suggested studying the designs of Chinese, Japanese, and Korean ware and their glazes. "The glaze on the foot of a Japanese piece will not be as fine as that of the Chinese." Sewell doesn't collect in his own field. "What I can afford doesn't meet my standards." How can anyone be satisfied with a five-hundred-dollar piece of porcelain when he is used to living with the one-hundred-fifty-thousand dollar pieces? But that's not your problem. You may not run into any Sung dynasty pieces, but "Semper Paratus" should be your motto. And if you are like most antiques detectives, while always on the lookout for rarities you can appreciate less expensive but finely done pieces.

Museum curator Jack Sewell casts his experienced eye on a fine Japanese Imari bowl with baked-on enameled decoration. "You wouldn't get a silhouette like this in a Chinese piece," he observes.

Are these marks Chinese reign marks or Japanese? The antiques detective would judge by more than the marks. The shape of the bowl and the design, as well as the blue in this blue and white piece, give clues. Everything except the marks seems Japanese. This is a perfect example of the Japanese use of Chinese characters. From the Art Institute of Chicago.

In this fine-quality blue and white Japanese plate, the painting is Japanese in feeling, even if you can't see the tones of the whites and blues. They would be further clues to its origins. From the Art Institute of Chicago.

You may have mixed feelings about Japanese porcelain from the Satsuma factories. The antiques detective can learn to recognize pieces with a fine crackling on the cream-colored surface. This museum-calibre vase shows a European influence in its brightly enameled, gilded figures. From the Art Institute of Chicago.

Indeed, there are probably more Oriental antiques to tempt collectors than any other variety. Unfortunately, many of them just got off the boat or were made to fill the needs of collectors in the 1920's and 1930's, when a house was not a home without something jade or ivory in it. Since then, the jade market has gone up and down, never quite reaching the high buying level of that era. Two good examples of porcelain that flooded the 20's market are the ubiquitous Rose Canton and Rose Medallion patterns, along with the gaudy and gilded versions of Satsuma made in Nagasaki, strictly for eager tourists and the export market. In this case, all that glitters certainly isn't gold and this ware is probably responsible for giving "made in Japan" items a bad reputation. To compound a collector's confusion, numerous blue and white porcelain patterns have been copied, adapted, and produced since the Ming Dynasty (1400-1600). Consider the popular Blue Willow pattern. It originated in England, was made in China, and today is made in Japan. If you didn't look at the backs of plates with similar patterns, would you know which was European, which Chinese, which Japanese? Or place two similar blue and white porcelain bowls side by side and try to decide which is Japanese, which is Chinese.

A little learning can be a dangerous thing for the Oriental collector. If a museum curator is sometimes unsure about Oriental objects, can an antiques detective always be certain? It may look Chinese, yet be Japanese. And to this point I have restricted my comments to porcelain and pottery.

You might begin your collection by reading about the philosophy of both the Chinese and Japanese cultures. Any insights gained will provide you with clues when you look at Oriental objects. The diverse philosophies are exhibited in their figurines. Chinese Kwan-Yin figures in white porcelain have a benign appearance; their expressions reflect serenity and kindness. The contrast between these "household" figures and those made for tombs and temples is considerable. The ferocious grimaces of the latter would frighten off any evil spirit—as they were meant to. Also compare designs decorating ceramic pieces. The Chinese subjects are delicately painted flowers, birds, and other themes from nature. Borders are usually geometric. Backgrounds are kept simple, so as not to distract from the central subject.

Now study some Japanese paintings and ceramics. The backgrounds are "busy" and lifelike. The men look like men, not gods. Scrutinize a piece of 19th-century export Imari porcelain or pottery. In the almost completely covered background, a complex of designs seems to run into one another in overglaze enamel colors of green, dark blues, reds, oranges and gold. Somehow the Japanese got the idea that Westerners liked ornate decorations, especially the overembellished Victorian styles. Ah, but don't think you can spot one of these plates and instantly say, "That's Imari!" The Chinese copied these popular designs.

To help you to identify the many types of Chinese ceramics, here are a few brief descriptions of some of them. *Blanc de Chine*—is a very fine white porcelain with a clear glaze, it varies in color from cream to chalk white and ofttimes rose tints. It was very popular around the turn of the 20th century

The shape is Japanese and the vase is early-18th-century Celadon Satsuma with an underglaze decoration. From the Art Institute of Chicago.

in Europe and America. Unlike ordinary white porcelain, it has no bluish or greenish tinge. When compared with the old, new Blanc de Chine shows stronger tones of gray, pink, and white. *Celadon ware*—was made in China, Japan, and Korea, its colors range from clear greens, blues, and browns to slightly off-colors in the same range. Some pieces were also discovered on islands in the South Pacific. *Sang de boeuf*—has a deep, reddish glaze that originated about the 17th century. Much of it has been made in the 20th century and turned into vases and lamp bases.

If you don't insist on having the fancy stuff you can find utilitarian wares—pottery ginger jars and food containers, primitive, attractive, and cheap. Most date from around 1870 to 1910, when they were used and then tossed away by the Chinese workers who helped build our railroads. Some

The bottle shape and long neck are clues to Japanese ceramics. On the left is a mid-17th-century Celadon, one of the earliest examples of Kakiemon porcelain and considered among the finest. At the right is an early Japanese Imari. The Kakiemon decorations were done in various combinations of underglazed blue and yellow, green, turquoise, and red. To identify an object as Japanese or Chinese is one of the true challenges for the antiques detective. From the Art Institute of Chicago.

have a handsome iridescent look from long burial. Their colors are usually greens, browns and yellows.

For a while there was a lot of blue and white porcelain, from the plum blossom ginger jars to the popular rice-pattern dishes, floating around in shops and at housesales. The rice-pattern dishes have rice-sized holes cut in the porcelain and are covered with an almost transparent greenish glaze. Some is overpriced because to the sellers it looked old. Some is underpriced because the sellers feel it should have "reign marks" to be worth anything. At one antique show on the east coast I spotted a booth filled with high-priced blue and white reproductions. Using my little knowledge and a lot of *déjà-vu,* I came to the conclusion they were reproductions, not recent, but nevertheless, of the 20th century. The dealer, who specialized in Oriental pieces, proudly explained he knew they were authentic because they had reign marks. Since he belongs to a small Oriental Collectors club, he should know better. It is not a question of his learning what some of the reign marks look like, but of his not learning that those fancy marks generally don't mean much. May I repeat that sentence, just in case you missed it? *Reign marks generally don't mean much.*

Considered in the famille verte *(green glaze enamel) category, this butterflies-and-cabbage pattern plate is also Chinese Export and probably dates from around the turn of the 20th century. The Chinese medallion in the center is gold and is not as commonly seen as the* famille rose *patterns.*

Most of the new pieces from Japan, especially the *famille rose* decorated ones, carry Ch'ien-lung marks. Many times the Japanese used Chinese "chop marks" on their blue and white pieces or made up some that looked as if they might be Chinese. In his books *Fakes*, Otto Kurz notes, "To say Ch'ing wares were faked in Europe from the 18th century onward would be an understatement." The dealer at the show apparently hadn't read about what he specialized in. He told me he would be opening a shop in England soon. He should do very well there—the English have been selling reproductions for a long, long time.

After a while, the experienced antiques detective doesn't worry whether a piece has a mark or not until it has passed other identity tests. He will say, however, "This can't be that period or that dynasty even though it has those marks, because the colors weren't in existence or those marks aren't in the right place for that historical time." That test requires you to memorize the reign marks important to your collection—if you still take stock in reign marks. Unless you read Chinese, this is quite a task. You may want to carry a little printed card that shows the reign marks of interest to you when you go searching.

To begin sifting clues for country of origin, look at the shape. If for instance, the object is an Oriental vase, does it have the traditional Chinese shape, short-necked and outwardly curving almost from the base of the neck? Or is it bottle-shaped with a long, thin neck? The bottle-shape is an important clue that it is typically Japanese. Next, consider the blue (if it is blue). Is it dark cobalt blue used in the Ming period or a similar, slightly brighter dark blue? Only by using the *déjà-vu* technique can the antiques detective say that the washed-out blue is Japanese or if the dark blue is Japanese or Chinese. Next, view the overall design. Does the pattern look blurred or have a dotted appearance? Are the figures in the picture godlike or relaxed and "doing their thing?" By now you are getting to know a little about Oriental philosophy and art and can recognize some subtle differences. Now look at the bottom. While the supposed expert would come to an instant decision upon sighting some chop marks or two blue rings around the base, you'll pass on to the next clue, won't you?

The antiques detective will carefully feel the piece, looking for the flaws and irregularities that could come only from an old kiln, not a modern factory. Even after you go through all this, the piece may still not be as old as it looks. But one consolation is that if after all that hocus-pocus, you still can't tell definitely what the piece dates to, neither can anyone else.

If there are no marks on a painted folding screen, no calligraphy whatsoever, how can you tell if the screen is Japanese, Chinese or Korean, much less its age? I don't know what the experts would suggest, but I do have such a problem. I have been living with a beautiful, faded, gold foil and painted screen for over a year. I still don't know too much about it. I found it lying in three sections on a basement floor. It was probably passed up because it had no obvious identifying marks. The price alone, five dollars, should have rated it a second glance. Visually taking it apart, I have come to a few con-

clusions. The only figure in the painting is a beautiful peacock with a suspicious look in his eye. There is no background to distract from the greens and blues of his body. The brush work is gracefully but strongly done. At this point I have two contrasting clues: (1) the lack of background is typically Chinese; (2) the boldness of the painting is Japanese in feeling. The back of the screen is covered with grey paper imprinted with bats. Bats are used symbolically in both Chinese and Japanese cultures. Because it has six panels, it is more likely to be Japanese. The Chinese use odd-numbered panels. The construction and joining of the panels offer another clue. The panels are joined by long strips of paper wrapped across the front of one panel and the back of the next, then likewise in the opposite direction, to make a secure hinge. From my research, I have learned this was a technique used until at least the middle of the 19th century. I will take a chance and say the screen is probably Japanese and of the Edo period (1615-1867). Whatever it is, for five dollars I have a piece of Oriental art that is different from the now popular screens coming in from Taiwan and Japan.

Another one of my unresolved riddles is that apparently Chinese chair belonging to my Scandinavian repairman. The mythological creature that

While this is undeniably a most unusual chair by today's standards, if you had attended the Philadelphia Centennial in 1876, you might have seen many like it, made in China for the United States market.

The details of this heavily carved chair show a mythological creature chomping on a flower. A dedicated antiques detective could probably make a final identification by tracking the source of the symbols.

Another type of furniture made for the eager United States market is this either rosewood or teak chair, heavily inlaid with mother-of-pearl (or plastic). Such Chinese Export pieces could have been made any time from 1880 to yesterday. Many antiques detectives have a hard time dating these ornate pieces.

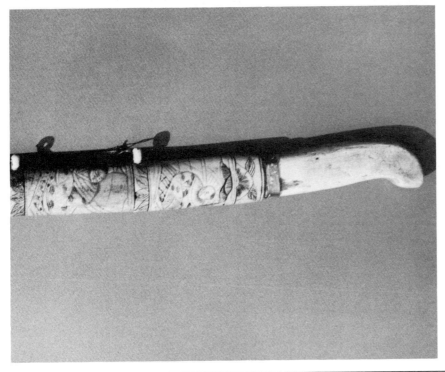

There is something about the sword case or "tsuba" that fascinates collectors of Oriental artifacts. Unfortunately, many of the swords have been sold piecemeal and the missing parts have been replaced with "antiqued" handles, guards, etc. Even in this black and white photo, a close look at this pseudo-samurai sword and tsuba should reveal three things. (1) The sword guard is missing. (2) The handle of the sword has been "antiqued" to look like old ivory or wood. Probably both of the missing parts have been sold to other collectors. (3) The case of carved ivory is cracked, probably on purpose either to make new ivory (from the 1920's) look ancient or to add authenticity to plastic. This does appear to be real ivory, however.

forms the chair looks like a prehistoric bird, deeply carved of teak with a wisteria flower in its beak and a mean look on its face. All of my Chinese experts say they have never seen anything like it. Recently, when doing some research on the Philadelphia Centennial, I came across some old *Harper's Magazines* with engravings of the various exhibits. From their descriptions of the Oriental displays, I would guess that the chair was made for the American market in 1876. And remembering the Chinese philosophy and their predeliction for mythological and godlike creatures, I would say the chair is Chinese. On the other hand....

Japanese swords are staging a comeback these days. Wondrous headlines in the Sotheby Parke Bernet newsletter proclaim sales in the thousands of dollars for single samurai swords. These aren't the 20th-century copies beloved by tourists traveling in Japan. By all appearances the SPB swords seem genuinely ancient. If you are a collector who has made a special trip to Japan in quest of your swords, I hope your zeal won't cause you to overlook any missing parts. For instance, the handle of the sword might once have been of ivory, but now it is of wood with an "antiqued" finish. You shouldn't get so carried away by the carved ivory figures on the "tsuba," or scabbard, that you ignore the fact that the ivory was broken and crudely patched. Old is old, but in this case, not necessarily old enough. Chances are the sword guard—a circle of iron or bronze, often decorated in silver and gold—is also missing. These guards are themselves collector's items. Do you carefully examine the sword blade itself for marks of hand-forging? Any early piece should be hand-forged. If you are an antiques detective, you must overcome any trace of glazed eyeball syndrome and systematically go over the piece, clue by clue.

An often overlooked source of early Chinese ceramics is the vase turned into a lamp, popular in the 1920's and revived in the 1970's. Some detectives have paid twenty dollars for a lamp at a garage sale and walked away with an early Chinese vase. Many fine vases were made into lamps that today are worth hundreds of dollars.

There are so many types of Oriental objects that it would be impossible for me to cover them all. But by now the antiques detective knows a few of the basics for detecting and differentiating and whether the items are textiles, lacquer or ceramics, he can apply his knowledge to determine age, origin, and authenticity.

6.
Looks Can Be Deceiving

Perhaps I have trained myself to see what others overlook.
—SHERLOCK HOLMES,
in *A Case of Identity*

Antiques can be confusing. An antique may look as if it were made by a certain craftsman known for his deft turnings or inlays, and may seem English or Scottish rather than American, yet the piece may have no "credential" to place it in its proper historical perspective. Who can say for certain that the small glass bottle with the enameled flowers and figures is or isn't the work of Baron William Henry Stiegel, 18th-century American glassmaker? It could, in fact, have been made in the 1900's in America or yesterday in West Germany. Naturally, the antique collector wants to be assured that the glass he is considering is "Stiegel," and the dealer wants to assure him. Whether you call it "origin by attribution" or "guilt by association," it's all covered by a vocabulary called "antiquese," by means of which an historical past is either subtly invented or assumed. The bottle will be referred to as "Stiegel-type" or the word "probably" will be used. "Probably Stiegel" sounds possible, doesn't it? When you see such a tentative attribution in an auction catalog or advertisement, your own mind can convince you the piece is authentic Stiegel. Once the thought is planted, it blossoms beautifully in your mind. More things are attributed to owners who probably never even saw them than you could imagine. You can't blame the dealers and auction houses for trying to make a living. They rightly figure the average buyer will be convinced that his purchase is really whatever "probably" says it is. The dealer, who may or may not know what the piece really dates to, figures nobody else does either. It's worth the chance to sell that glass bottle or bowl that looks like a much-wanted antique for twice as much, as if it had a pedigree. The dogged antiques detective has to wade through the antiquese and decide for himself what the piece really is, no matter if Mrs. Upton Upyours

85

At first glance, this small tumbler with blue and yellow enamel flowers could be a "Stiegel" type, at least to a beginning glass collector, but the antiques detective would doubt that conclusion. The design of the flowers and the shape of the glass point to the 19th century. Some bubbles in the glass, indicating early manufacture, aren't sufficient proof. Later, at an antique show, the antiques detective spots a "water set," pitcher and matching tumblers, exactly like the single tumbler. Seen in the context of the total set, the tumbler is late-Victorian.

owned a bottle that is *probably* Stiegel. All that concerns him is, is it or isn't it?

Keep in mind that when the object is sold with that modifying "probably" in front of its name, the dealers and auctions houses are off the hook. They "think" the piece appears to be "of the Queen Anne period." If it turns out not to be, you can't fault them. The fancier auction houses even offer lengthy explanations of "antiquese" in the front of their brochures. In the grip of auction fever, however, many bidders forget what was clearly explained. The average antique buyer hears the florid words describing his prize as he wants to hear them.

If you are a lover of early American glass, your research tools should include books on the subject, auction catalogs when the sale deals with the 18th- and early-18th-century American glass, and side trips to the museums that are either near or on the actual site of the early glass houses. The following few brief case histories may help you with your own deductions.

Case History of Some Glass Objects

Many antiques detectives have gotten glassy-eyed trying to "psych out" a piece of unidentified glass. Have you ever tried to count the ribbing on a small plate or bottle? These "ribs" fan out from the pontil mark and curve around it. They are often so minute, you can get cross-eyed trying to count them, but count you must if you are to decide whether it came from this or that glass factory. Perhaps you have just spied a small glass object in a junk shop in Sheboygan, Wisconsin. Whether it was originally a small drinking glass or a jar, you can't tell yet. In fact, you are tempted to pass it up because of its bright apple-green color. Anything that bright can't be very old. Nevertheless, the color does catch your eye and you pick the glass up. The shopkeeper helpfully suggests it is probably Mexican. The price is two dollars and fifty cents.

Clue 1: The first thing collectors of early glass look for is a pontil, or mold mark. Its appearance offers a clue to the piece's age and origin. This piece has a small, rough pontil and so do modern Mexican-made pieces. However, most of the Mexican pieces are filled with bubbles and overall have a crude appearance. They are also a little heavy. This piece is lightweight, almost fragile.

Clue 2: The glass is slightly under three inches high, and barrel-shaped. When tapped lightly with a pen, it emits the bell-like ring found in early glass. At this point it would be very easy to rely on "antiquese" and say, "probably early glass." But for the antiques detective, this is only the beginning.

Clue 3: When you get the glass home, you begin a careful scrutiny with your magnifying glass. Not only are the ribs very narrow, but some expanded vertical ribs criss-cross through the concentric ribs. Past research has taught you that this type of glass was made in the Connecticut valley and is sometimes known as "Pitkin," after the Pitkin glass works in Connecticut.

A barrel-shaped tumbler in apple-green glass doesn't look very old at first glance. Going beyond the color and shape, the antiques detective concentrates on the narrow ribbing that swirls around the glass. When the glass is held to the light, expanded vertical ribs are seen, swirling in the opposite direction. A fellow glass collector feels positive it is European glass, certainly not American. Why not? Well, for one thing, it isn't his discovery. For another, who would ever find a piece of early American glassware in Sheboygan, Wisconsin, for a couple of dollars?

A closeup of the base of the tumbler shows that it is mold-blown and that the ribbing swirls to the right, typical of several types of American glass made from 1800 to the 1830's. Is it American or European? I don't know. Do you?

The double-pattern in spiraling vertical swirls and the ribbing that turns left is typical of Pitkin pieces. If it is really Pitkin, it could date from 1783 to 1830. It could also be from the middle 19th century, made by the Boston & Sandwich Glass Company, who did similar pieces. Or it could be a product of the midwest at that same period. In any case, the bright apple-green color is still a puzzle.

Clue 4: Still researching, you come across another possibility in the book, *American Glass,* by George and Helen McKearnin. There were a number of glass houses in the Midwest which copied the Stiegel style. One of them, in Zanesville, Ohio, was noted for the thinness of its glass, and made items known today as "Ohio Stiegel," as did factories in Kent and Mantua. Pictures of small tumblers are similar to the piece.

Clue 5: Still thumbing through the McKearnin book, you spot another similarly shaped piece described as a "spinning bowl," used in the 19th century. It was filled with water and used to dampen the flax as the woman spun. The pictures showed glasses from two and three-quarter to three inches high.

Deduction: Not having any positive identification, the antiques detective has to stick her neck out and say that it appears to be midwestern mid-19th-century American. Whether it is a small tumbler or "spinning bowl" remains a mystery. A couple of dollars isn't bad for an attractive example of early-19th-century American glass and the case isn't closed yet. The antiques detective never closes the files on an unsolved mystery.

Some common clues for common glass may be helpful to the collecting sleuth. When beginning collectors think of antique glass, they generally don't think about most of it as being everyday glassware for 18th- and 19th-century families. Today's heavy drinking glasses picked up as gas station premiums or at MacDonald's are our version of the heavy tumblers our grandparents used. Of course, much antique glass is beautifully etched and cut and of light weight. But much of what you may be ignoring is glass *ordinaire,* by now antique. The glass used in the hotels, restaurants and on steamboats of the 19th century was heavy but attractive everyday glass. The riverboat pieces can be identified by their heavy bottoms that kept them from sliding around. These and many other utility pieces were "pillar-moulded"; the exterior of the glass was swirled or vertically corrugated and the interior was smooth. Much of it was made in the United States, in the Pittsburgh and Wheeling glass houses. The compote shown here looks at first as it was supposed to, like heavy lead crystal, especially the stem. A variant of lead crystal developed in the middle of the 19th century by Hobbs, Bruckunier and Company in Wheeling, West Virginia, and known as "lime" glass, it was cheaper to make than lead glass and perfect for everyday use. Like lead glass, it has a deep bell tone when tapped. The clue to its origins is the combination of heavy, pattern-molded foot with the "cut" stem. While it isn't the fanciest molded glass, it is a good example for checking out glass clues. You'll be amazed at the number of collectors and dealers who don't recog-

This compote first appears to be lead crystal. Certainly the base has the look of cut crystal and when tapped, the piece has a nice ring. In his ongoing search for clues, the antiques detective is confused by the fact that the piece is molded, but research reveals this is "lime" glass, a cheap substitute for lead glass, made in the middle 19th century for use as everyday glassware.

nize glass made by Pittsburgh and Wheeling glass houses. This makes it all the better for you to build up a collection inexpensively now.

This goblet is one of four I inherited from my grandmother years ago. Notice the similarity of its heavy footed base and the "cut" stem to the compote. The fern design was done by copper-wheel engraving. For many years I have been looking for more of its mates at every antique show that came to town. Surprisingly, until recently none of the dealers knew much about the pattern or the date of the glasses. Backtracking to that junk shop in Sheboygan, Wisconsin, I found four goblets, similar but not exact matches to my grandmother's goblets. Priced at three and a half dollars each, they were a good buy. And they could be mixed and matched to form a set of eight. I still don't know where they were made. But by placing them beside the compote, I have been able to deduce they are the same "lime" glass and may date from the late 19th century. Just like the compote, they ring like lead crystal. Next time you see a piece that both does and doesn't look like lead crystal, your *déjà-vu* will identify it as "lime" glass.

The antiques detective places this beautifully shaped goblet with copper-wheel-engraved fern pattern and cut stem next to the compote and comes up with another example of "lime" glass.

At first glance, with its painted surface this small lady's desk appears to be 1920's French revival. The painting is in the manner of Angelica Kauffmann, who did similar furniture decoration in the 18th century and had many imitators.

Case History of a Fancy French Escritoire

At first sight this small desk looks like a piece of 1920's ersatz painted French furniture. In fact, for a long time, many of my collecting friends snubbed it. I myself hadn't paid much attention to it since it had come through my front door along with other inherited antiques years ago. For lack of space, the desk was placed in the entry hall behind the front door. Once in a while it got dusted.

One day as I was looking about the house for another antique to photograph for this book, my eye came to rest on the neglected desk. Dragging it from behind the door to a sunny place, I began to examine it carefully. First, I saw it in outline form. It did indeed have the lines of a Louis XV piece, with its cabriole legs and bronze-shod feet. Next, I gazed at it with its details "filled in." It was painted with a pale green lacquer. A delicate landscape with a man and a woman in period fashions of the 18th century was painted on the drop front. Floral decorations were painted on the sides and top. The two front legs terminated in ornate bronze mounts and the keyhole had a rococo bronze escutcheon.

Clue 1: When I opened the slant top and examined the lock, I discovered it was steel. Judging by the fact there were no other indentations where a larger lock might once have been (which is common with early pieces), I judged this to be the original. Locks on 18th- and early-19th-century pieces were steel and iron. The hinges appeared to be original.

Examine this detail of the drawer lock, which appears to be the original.

The interior of the desk shows warping of drawers and shrinkage of various sections. The drawer bottoms are rough and unfinished.

A side view of the drawer shows the wide dovetails, typical of those in the 18th century.

Clue 2: Removing one of the interior drawers, I observed the wide dovetailing of both front and back of the drawer, another detail typical of the 18th century. Turning the drawer over, I looked through my magnifying glass at the saw marks, which showed the jagged lines of frame or pit saws used in the 18th century. Shrinkage and warping, quite proper for a two-hundred-year-old piece of furniture, had pulled the drawers away from the sides of the drawer compartments. Drawer bottoms were rough, unfinished.

Clue 3: With much huffing and puffing I turned the small but heavy piece upside down to examine tool marks and workmanship. Once again, I found the early saw marks, a few handwrought nail heads and a totally

The bottom of the desk shows wide boards, still rough and unfinished, proper for an 18th-century piece. The saw marks are visible, showing the jagged lines of 18th-century saws. From the styling and construction clues, we can deduce that the piece is a late-18th- or early-19th-century French escritoire.

rough, unfinished surface. The case itself was made of mahogany. The drawers were a combination of mahogany for the front, and a wood, strange to me, making up the rest of the drawer.

Deduction: The desk was made in the late 18th to early 19th century. Though it appears to be French in the Louix XV style, looks can be deceiving. Its decorative painting is similar to that done by an artist of the period, Angelica Kauffmann, whose work was much copied for years after it was fashionable. Now I not only dust the desk regularly, but have placed it at the head of the stairs for doubters to see and ponder.

Use your sense of déjà-vu *on this chest of drawers. Look at it in bare outline, without the paint job and hardware. The shape is transitional between Chippendale-apron and heavy Empire form. The painted designs and fruit handles are late Victorian. Only the interior of the piece offers true clues to its age, which shows you can't judge an antique by its paint job. The deduction is that the chest was made anywhere from 1830 on.*

Case History of a Painted Chest

If you've priced 19th-century painted American furniture lately, you know things have gotten out of hand. Even worse, you can see many recently painted pieces, passing as old. A chest of drawers or a dressing table with an original paint job can cost you two hundred dollars and up in a shop. No wonder that I was surprised to find what looked like a mid-Victorian chest of drawers at a basement sale for only twenty dollars. Before I begin this case history, let us take a long, hard look at the chest. The base color is ochre and the designs are done in dark brown. The paint job is a combination of free hand and stencils. When I came face-to-face with the chest, I experienced a strong sense of *déjà-vu*. I had seen a picture of a similar chest in an out-of-print book on Victorian antiques, along with the statement that many antique collectors wouldn't realize that the chest was an early painted one, originally sold by one of the mail order houses around the turn of the century. If this twenty-dollar chest was a mail-order-catalog antique, that lopped a hundred dollars off its value. But whatever it was, for the price it offered good storage space with its four roomy drawers. When I got it home, I hurried to the library to find the reference book I had remembered. Thumbing through its pages, I found my chest or at least a chest with a similar paint job. The rest of the chest wasn't quite the same as its catalog cousin. Once again, I had to play detective.

Clue 1: Ignoring the design, I looked at the silhouette of the chest. It seemed to be an early- or first-quarter-of-the-19th-century style. The bracket feet and scalloped apron were leftovers and adaptations of country Chippendale.

Clue 2: Taking out the drawer, I found it made of pine with a walnut bottom. The drawer was double-dovetailed. The bottom of the drawer was rough and showed the jagged marks of the frame or pit saw. The lock on the drawer was steel and appeared to be the original one. Behind the drawer pulls, with their carved fruit motif, were screw holes each of which could also have secured a turned wooden knob at one time. Peering inside the case with a flashlight, I noted the sides were made of wide boards. One on each side was, however, a later addition. While the rest of the piece was pine, they were walnut and bore circular saw marks.

Clue 3: Looking at the back of the chest, I again observed the widely cut boards. Here, too, the walnut had circular saw marks, while the pine had frame saw lines. I looked again at the boards inside to make sure the pine boards showed the early saw marks.

Deduction: This is an American country chest, originally made anywhere from 1830 on. The paint job and the Victorian fruit pulls were added later to make the piece "stylish." The rather heavy appearance of the chest shows the earlier Empire influence.

If the piece had been a factory-made catalog piece, the drawers might not have been dovetailed at all or the dovetails would have been uniformly spaced and of the same size. The boards, of course, would have been of one size and would probably have been planed smooth.

Is it really as elementary as it seems? Keep in mind that there are exceptions to many antique rules.

These last photographs illustrate some good examples of how "looks can be deceiving."

Ask yourself where have you seen this desk before. What is wrong with it in outline appearance? Antiques detective-owner, Malcom Dunn, discovered it once had ball feet. The keyhole escutcheon (not visible) in the slant top and the brasses are 19th-century. Behind the pigeonholes is a secret compartment. Dunn's step-by-step deductions and research prove the desk to be late-17th-century and Irish.

A pair of 18th-century Venetian mirrors were found by an antiques detective in a Lake Forest, Illinois, garage. The owner had just inherited them along with other antiques, but preferred contemporary décor. Notice the deep, etched appearance of the male figure and the border. By now the antiques detective can recognize the effect achieved by copper-wheel engraving. Upon taking the mirror apart, the antiques detective notices its surface has the look of tin foil, rather than the look of "silvering." Until around 1840, a sheet of tin foil and a quantity of mercury were combined for mirror plates used primarily in Europe. So this mirror plate has a right to look like tin foil. Another clue to the age of the mirror is the lozenge shape, popular in the 18th century.

The back of the frame shows the uneven marks of the early saws. There have been many reproductions of these Italian mirrors, but based on the clues, the antiques detective concludes they are late-18th- to middle-19th-century Italian.

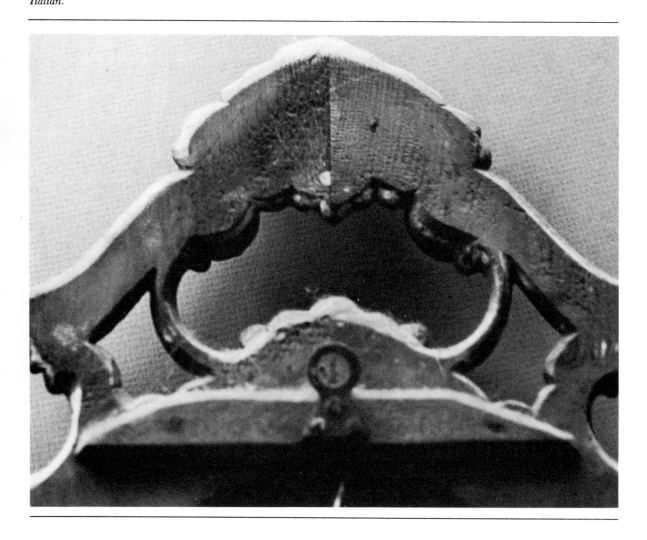

This may be a canary yellow Sandwich glass whale oil lamp, now converted to a table lamp.

Do you know your pontil marks? The bottle on the left was made before 1840; the pontil is rough cut. The pressed pontil on the right belongs to a faked Jenny Lind flask, made around 1905.

This bottle is attributed to the Zanesville, Ohio, glass factory. Swirls and collared lip are clues that matched it with similar bottles in the McKearnin book on glass. Others ignored it at a well-attended housesale, even though it was priced at just four dollars. It is now worth many hundreds of dollars.

Here's an unusual item—a tuck-away table. It is fashioned in the simplified style of many Shaker pieces. Note the circular saw marks on the upturned base.

Of three different types of glass, all are Sandwich (or Sandwich-type). The plate on the left is probably Midwestern, in a lacy pattern; the miniature lacy cup and saucer, of Eastern origin; master salt dip, also Eastern, pictured in Ruth Webb Lee's Sandwich Glass Handbook. *Would you recognize each of them to be Sandwich or Sandwich-type?*

7.
Try the Lineup

And now if we pass on to the second point, we find that each throws light upon the other.

—SHERLOCK HOLMES,
in *The Adventure of the Stockbroker's Clerk*

There's nothing like a lineup to identify an elusive antique. Side by side, differences in style and materials stand out. Some antiques detectives keep a scrapbook of photos of similar antiques from antique trade publications and auction catalogs. But you must be sure that the photos are correctly identified in the first place, or false information will be passed on. I keep a scrapbook of color photos of Oriental rugs, which gives me clues to the various colors and designs, along with dates and characteristics. I also have photos of everything I collect. When I find similar pieces, I pull out the photos and compare them with the new object. Who has time for all of this? You can even do it while watching TV or listening to the stereo.

Let's begin with one of the most common antiques, the *country chair,* both slat-back and spindle-back varieties. At first glance they may all look alike, but when you line up several, they immediately show small but important differences. This can be especially important if you are shopping for the earliest examples at country auctions or thrift shops. The 19th-century plank-bottom varieties were usually made of pine and maple, or combinations of woods. The antiques detective knows that no matter how icky the paint job, underneath luscious, mellow wood waits to be revived. Some of the new paint removers don't remove the original wood surface. Or you can paint over the existing bad paint job with one of the antiquing kits on the market. Spindle-back chairs were meant to be painted. They are the poor man's version of the "fancy chairs," painted and stenciled beginning around 1825 by such manufacturers as Lambert Hitchcock. Hitchcock

Can you find and date the oldest chair in this group of plank-bottom chairs? Until recently you could find and buy any of them for a couple of dollars apiece. Now they are being rediscovered and repainted in the style of the 19th century. The oldest is on the far left, a thumb-back Windsor type, probably made around 1830 or 1840. The third from the left, with the wide back, was probably a kitchen work chair or a variant of a child's chair. The legs have not been cut down.

A good example of a thumb-back Windsor after refinishing. It was purchased "in the rough" from the stripper and now has a new front rung. Many of these chairs are now showing up newly painted and stenciled and sold for seventy-five to a hundred dollars each, as having original paint.

chairs were the first mass-produced American chairs. Backs, seats and other parts were made on an assembly-line basis and when put together, the chairs were painted and stenciled in the same way. As their name implies, they were fancier than their country cousins. Legs and spindles were artfully turned in a variety of styles, seats were caned or covered with woven rush or painted wood. The country adaptations varied from region to region. When you place them side by side after researching regional characteristics, you may be able to say, "That one is from the East" or "It is from the Midwest." Some of the finer versions are known as Country Windsors. Time was when the antiques detective could buy enough at two dollars each to

Would you recognize this as a late-18th-century English Windsor? Another dealer rescued it from a fire in an antique shop and sold it to me for ten dollars. The soot was removed, without damaging the original surface. With my wood chart's help, I identified the wood as "zebra." Notice the graining in the seat. The split-turning on the legs and seat give evidence of its age. Notice the warping of the round seat. Turned upside down, the rough seat shows marks of the early gash saw.

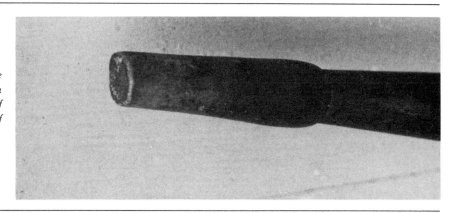

Notice the wear mark on the worn foot—that's what you should expect to find on the leg of a chair that has had a couple of hundred years of use.

have a breakfast table grouping. That may still be possible, but not all at one time. Today's going price can be as much as twenty-five dollars for a graceful example, even covered with layers of paint. Check out your local stripping shop for discoveries. I have been lucky enough to find interesting unclaimed chairs for as little as four dollars for an early-19th-century low-back Windsor, or "firehouse Windsor."

I regret that I haven't come across any 17th-century slat-back chairs to line up in photographs. Those laying claim to being that old show up at the fanciest antique shows for over one thousand dollars each. I wish I could find one in someone's garage, but the closest I have come is to discover an 18th-century English Windsor at a warehouse sale for ten dollars. The sellers informed me it had been one of the pieces saved during a fire in an antique shop. Because the surface was blackened with soot and they probably thought it couldn't be salvaged, the price was low. Little did they know what a little elbow grease can do. The chair is unusual because the seat is round, warped but round. It is very thick and the underside is unfinished. It shows the marks of the early pit saw. The back legs are worn at the foot and the front rung is uneven from wear. Even the antiques detective who can afford the thousand dollars per chair should do some investigating before putting out cash. The wood should be typical of the woods used in that period; the backs and finials, if any, should be worn and warped. If only a rung shows wear, it is not enough of a clue to count. Think about how you move a chair around. What receives the most wear? If they have been dragged across old wooden floors dozens of times, the back legs should be uneven. The turnings should show some signs of the concentric rings left by early lathes. The antiques detective looks for and values signs of wear. The uninformed buyer looks for and values a piece that looks brand-new, and it probably is. The antiques detective is suspicious of a piece that looks too good, unless it has been restored for display in a museum.

A lineup of *brass candlesticks* can give at least a first impression of age and design, as well as place of origin. The oldest candlestick shown here is the one with the pricket (left, back row). The wide rim on top was used to catch the drippings and is of the type used in the 17th century. Its baluster

A lineup of candlesticks of varying ages and origins reveals many clues. The shape of the tall stick at the left of the back row and the pricket would tell the antiques detective it is probably a 17th- or early-18th-century church piece from the middle or far East. The middle stick has the classic lines of the English Adam period. The stick on the right with its wide saucer and socket top is characteristic of both the late 17th century and 19th century. The shape is more French or Italian than anything else. The chamberstick at the left in the front row is a push-up type, used from the 1840's on. The small chamberstick with a baluster turning and wide saucer is typical of early-19th-century styles. The antiques detective can distinguish differences in shape and style with this method of comparison.

stem is also of the 17th-century type. The country of origin remains a mystery. A variety of experts have suggested everywhere from China to Russia and Europe. The candlestick in the middle of the back row is the vase-shaped, neo-classical style of the end of the 18th century. Its base is still wide enough to catch the wax drippings. Judged by its shape alone, it could be English. The candlestick (far right, back row) has a nicely turned baluster stem and a wide drip base. Instead of a simple lip, it has a socket inside and the outer lip is turned over, features characteristic of the late 17th century and also found in the 19th century. This is a good example of why the antiques detective can't make a snap judgment on the basis of a single clue. The thin chamberstick in the front row, left, has a design stamped into the base and a push-up device to keep moving up the burning candle. This is a stlye from the 1840's. The chamberstick on the right shows the baluster turning and wide saucer base common to the 19th-century pieces.

If he hasn't already done so, the antiques detective will tap the candlesticks to make sure they are pure brass. Many reproductions don't ring. The candlestick on the far right has a bell-like ring when tapped and a pinkish cast to the metal, two qualities found in bellmetal. Because of the large copper content, bellmetal objects can be recognized by their slightly pink cast. They are highly prized because not many bellmetal candlesticks were cast and few survive from the early 19th century.

The large pricket stick shows the concentric rings of early lathe turning. It has deeply cut rings that are an attempt at decoration. It comes apart and is hollow. I bought it from a woman who had several pieces of jewelry which had belonged to a Czar including a locket with his painted portrait and a lock of his hair. Is the candlestick really Russian? Where did the now deceased owner find it? How did it arrive in Chicago? There's a mystery to haunt any antiques detective!

Next, the antiques detective looks at the construction of the candlestick. Was it cast or spun? All of the candlesticks except the chamberstick in the left foreground were cast. Because they were finished on one of the early lathes, their lathe marks, concentric lines, can still be seen on the bases. The chamberstick on the left was made of sheet brass. The design was then die-struck. It is much thinner and lighter in weight than the cast pieces. Both the pricket stick and the vase-shaped stick show evidence of being sandcast in the pebbly, rough surface of their bases.

This silver-plated candlestick was offered at a private housesale as "maybe 18th century." The owner had bought it in the 1930's as an antique. Assuming you know nothing whatsoever about what an 18th-century candlestick looks like, try the lineup test. When the silver-plated candlestick is seen next to the authenticated "Tiffany bronze" candlestick, even an amateur can notice the similarity of their design. The silver-plated piece isn't a signed Tiffany, but is a crude attempt to take advantage of the prevailing fashion around the end of the 19th century for Tiffany-styled objects. It may not be a thing of beauty, but it does hold a candle.

This closeup of a sheet-brass chamberstick shows the detail of the stamped design.

Try the lineup technique on this pewter candlestick, sold at a housesale as "maybe 18th century."

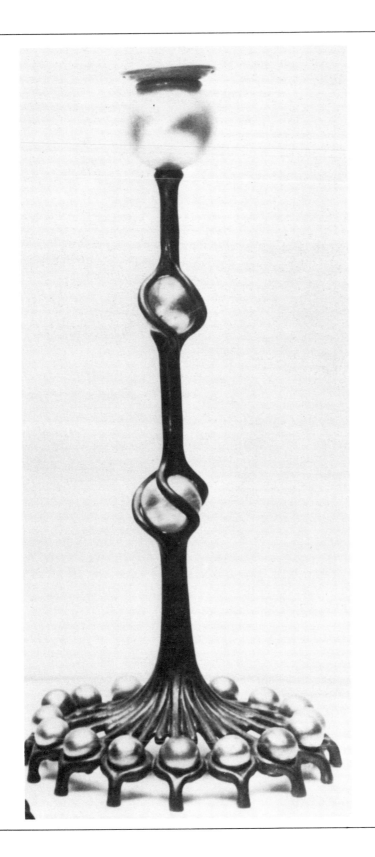

Notice a similarity in silhouette between this Tiffany candlestick and the crude pewter version. Both are from the turn of the 20th century.

Line up three blue and white Oriental bowls. Their designs and shapes should tell antique detectives that only one is Chinese and that the other two are Japanese. But which?

Try a lineup of *Oriental bowls* like the three shown here. The first thing the antiques detective will notice is a slight difference in their shape as well as in their design. If the photograph were in color, you would also see three different shades of blue. You could also observe that the bowl on the left and the one in the center are hand-painted, while the bowl on the right is a transfer print. A small amount of research will tell you that two of the bowls are middle-19th-century Japanese and one is late-18th-century Chinese. But which?

Turned over, the same three bowls might confuse some antiques detectives. The transfer print bowl on the right has a chop mark and a reign mark. Is it Chinese after all? The bowl on the left has the geometric border typical of Japanese pottery.

Backtracking a bit, you'll notice that the center bowl is typically Chinese in shape. The other two are Japanese in feeling. The center bowl shows the Chinese simplified treatment of a floral design. If this were Japanese, there would be more flowers, leaves and designs. The bowl on the left shows figures that appear human, not godlike, a Japanese attitude. The painting has

a blurred look, characteristic of Japanese attempts to mimic Chinese painting, though the genuine Chinese work didn't look blurry. Despite its phony reign mark, the bowl on the right is a Japanese transfer print and an example of Japanese copy work. Again, if you could see the bowls in color, you would notice the greenish cast of the white porcelain. Here is more proof that the lineup can be a good way to train your eye for instant detections at auction previews.

A lineup of *soup tureens* is a real test of an antiques detective's savvy. Without ever looking for marks or being concerned with material, the detective can closely date a soup tureen. Whether of ceramic or of silver, their shapes are distinctive to their periods. I am not referring to the animal and fowl shapes, but to the basic deep bowl. The shape of the ironstone tureen is characteristic of America-Empire period, which places it around 1830. The shape of the silver tureen is typical of the neo-classic forms of the late 18th century. How do I know so much about soup tureens? I got help from a handsome book on the subject put out by the Campbell Museum. I studied the photographs and observed the shapes from round to oval. The ceramic

Try the Lineup   117

pieces followed the fashions of the silver pieces of each era. The earliest known come from the end of the 17th century. The tureen lineup would show the various design motifs. The acanthus leaf design with gold trim on the handles of the ironstone piece is an example of very simple classic design, typical of Empire fashion in decoration. The rectangular shape of the ironstone piece was popular in America in the 19th century. The strawberry finial is found in other fruit and flower forms in this upright position in 18th-

century silver hollow ware. Even though both tureens have a similar finial trim, their shapes define their historical ages. If a tureen were Victorian from the middle of the 19th century, its shape would be totally different and the design of a ceramic piece might include a transfer print with an historical view (especially early 19th century). Even a plain white stoneware tureen with no design or marks whatsoever would be at least partially identifiable as to date by its shape.

A *bottle* lineup is pretty tricky for a novice, but can be simplified if he knows how glassmaking evolved and bottles changed over the years. The first thing apparent in the bottle lineup is the variety of body shapes. That is clue one. Clue two is the way the lips (tops) of the bottles finished off. Your third clue would be the colors of the bottles.

The oldest bottle is the one with the asymmetrical shape, second from the right. This lack of rigid form tells the antiques detective it was free-blown or handblown. It is typical of the form blown from 1820 to 1830. The sloping shoulders and sloping collared lip were new at the time. The flask on the far right shows the seam up the side as a result of being blown in a mold. Without seeing the pictures of Jackson on one side and Washington on the other, the detective would gauge its age by where the seam stops on the bottle and by its shirred lip and could come up with a date of around 1830. Both this bottle and the free-blown one have rough pontil marks. Since portrait flasks went out of vogue in 1850, the bottle must have been made prior to that. The portrait bottle is a dark olive green. The free-blown bottle is a lighter olive green. The flask second from left with the seam going up to the top of the shoulder is also mold-blown. The lip is applied and the pontil mark is smooth. These three clues would tell the detective the bottle was made around 1850. You may note that the shape is slightly different than that of the two bottles to its right. The eagle motif is typical of the series of flasks done in America in the middle of the 19th century. The color is pale aquamarine, considered a common, not a rare color. The long-necked bottle has a totally different look in regards to shape. The mold seam goes all the way up the neck to the lip. The base of the bottle is squared off, as was customary late in the 19th century. The color is light amber. The pontil is smooth. All of these bottles are American-made. The earlier ones are pictured in *American Glass,* by George and Helen McKearnin. The eagle flask was passed up at a housesale. Because of its smooth pontil, the dealers probably weren't sure whether or not it was a reproduction. Many otherwise knowledgeable dealers can't differentiate old from new historical flasks. Their ignorance gives me and you a better chance. Bottles would make a good subject for a photo scrapbook file if you are just beginning to collect. Studying the file, you could learn to recognize the oldies by their shape and the way they were made.

Would you believe Depression glass can resemble Sandwich glass? Make your own deductions from this Depression glass plate, known to collectors as Wildflower and by other names. Made by the Indiana Glass Company, it is Sandwich style, No. 618. It does not ring when thumped.

*This rare lacy Sandwich glass
bowl, made around 1840, has a
beautiful bell tone when tapped.
Courtesy, Allan J. Hodges.*

Which is the oldest andiron? The shapes and designs are clues. The brass fire dog on the left is a reproduction of an early-19th-century andiron. The cast iron on the right dates from around 1920. A close look at its design shows an Art Deco influence.

Can you decide when these trivets were made? Both were found in decaying Victorian frames in the "bottom of a barrel." The one on the left is not a reproduction, but a Victorian-period trivet. Rather than stripping the yellow paint that originally covered it, it has been repainted. The heart-shape on the right is handwrought, the underside does show some tool marks, and the bottom or the feet some wear, but somehow it doesn't seem as old as it is supposed to. I suspect that it is a 19th-century reproduction of an earlier handwrought iron trivet.

8.
The Importance of Marksmanship

Chance has put in our way a most singular and whimsical problem, and its solution is its own reward.

—SHERLOCK HOLMES,
in *The Man with the Twisted Lip*

It is an absolute necessity for the "carriage trade" dealer to stock a good supply of signed pieces for the mark-happy antique buyer. Marksmanship is a very important part of antique gamesmanship. Since you never know when a friend will turn over that vase or that silver bowl, it had better have the "right" marks from Tiffany to Bateman or the reputation of your status collection can go right down the drain. Generally, the same people who must carry their *LV-* or *G*-marked shopping bags to the supermarket are the first to turn over demitasse cups and silver, searching for marks. Just as "everybody knows" LV stands for Louis Vuitton and G for Gucci, so do some antique buyers think that crossed swords are a guarantee of Meissen and that Ming marks on porcelain are a guarantee of Ming period objects. In their zeal for the status antique, they may overlook the fact that such an ugly vase could never have come from the Sevres factory, or that the awkward, over-decorated piece of silver could not have been made by a Georgian silversmith. After all, the vase has the proper mark and the silver has Georgian hallmarks.

A mark is often the last thing the antiques detective is concerned with, just one of a myriad of clues to be considered. A mark can even throw the antiques detective off the scent. Because a piece of porcelain looks Chinese and has the identifying red seal mark doesn't mean it isn't a recent reproduction or one made by the famous forger Samson of Paris. An antiques detective must recognize the difference in the brush strokes of European artists and the delicate strokes of Chinese artists.

The antiques detective knows, too, that some very important antique items have no marks at all and that he must learn to recognize them when others pass them by. Even if a piece is unmarked, once it is authenticated as being Tiffany or any other big name, it will have the same or close to the same market value as the marked piece. When the time comes to sell it, the authenticated unmarked item will have *more* value than the marked reproduction or marked outright fake. Time has a way of catching up with fakes. While an identification mark on an authentic object is always important, it's cheaper and more rewarding to discover a valuable piece without marks.

What stops most collectors from doing their own research is a lack of time. There is nothing simple about tracing a mark or the history of marks. It involves going over page after page of similar marks in the many available reference books. When an object has no mark or signature on the back, the antiques detective has to find some other means of identification: shape, color, material, and style.

One of the most popular American ceramics is *Staffordshire* decorated with American historical scenes. Earliest and hardest to come by, as well as most expensive, is the dark blue transfer print made from 1818 to 1830. While some pieces have the name of the potter on the bottom, others don't. The antiques detective will consult a book, *American Historical Views of Staffordshire China*, by Ellouise Baker Larsen, that makes identification of

The border offers the essential clue as to the maker of this Staffordshire plate. The antiques detective first notes the color of the Staffordshire. If it is the early dark blue, he will next check out the border design in American Historical Views of Staffordshire China.

the pieces easy. You simply match the various decorative borders on the pieces illustrated with the borders on your items. The potters may have done similar scenes but never copied one another's border designs. For instance, Enoch Wood and Sons used shells. But when the mark became E.W. & S., the border design changed too and a flower and fruit pattern was used. James and Ralph Clews used buds, scrolls, and roses. All of the pictures on these pieces show views executed by well-known artists of the period. The early dark blues were followed by such colors as green, light blue, and purple. Those English potters really knew how to make a dollar; they offered Americans subjects from their recent historical past, as well as contemporary scenes. Some of the scenes were taken from "Picturesque Views Series," by the artist W. G. Wall, published in the *Hudson River Portfolio*. By checking the border book, any antiques detective could quickly identify the plate "Hudson River Views" as one made by James Clews between 1829 and 1836.

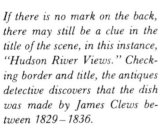

If there is no mark on the back, there may still be a clue in the title of the scene, in this instance, "Hudson River Views." Checking border and title, the antiques detective discovers that the dish was made by James Clews between 1829–1836.

Where an object turns up, marked or unmarked, isn't a clue to anything. Can you believe a *Sevres-marked bowl* in Honolulu? While lecturing in Hawaii, I was called by a collector to help date and identify some of her things. She had been picking up antiques over the last twenty years, either because they appealed to her or because they were inexpensive. She discovered a Georgian teapot in a Honolulu alley, discarded because the owner didn't want to remove layers of tarnish. The collector stored her antiques in a hall closet for years, until one day she decided to sell them if they had any value. The large bowl she showed me appeared to be of the type made in Sevres, France, in the 18th century and not the sort of piece to lie neglected in a closet. Sevres, when authentic, is found in museums and in the collections of the super rich. This hardpaste porcelain is most recognizable in pieces with paintings enclosed in panels of vivid blues, pinks and yellows. Also typically Sevres are festoons of flowers, such as characterized the Honolulu bowl, which rested on a bronze footed base. So far it had the characteristics of an 18th-century Sevres piece. I turned it over to reveal the famous Sevres factory mark, crossed *L*'s with a date letter enclosed. *Chaffer's Dictionary of Pottery and Porcelain Marks* showed the corresponding date letter to be 1770. The mark appeared genuine. If genuine, this closet bowl would be worth over a thousand dollars according to current market prices.

Unless you are familiar with the decorations and form of Sevres porcelain, you can't know its age or origin by just looking at the pastel-colored decorations.

The crossed L *'s with the date letter in the middle would send an antiques detective to* Chaffer's Dictionary of Pottery and Porcelain Marks, *where the piece is identified as French Sevres, ca. 1770.*

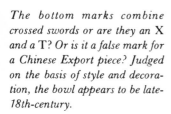

These small hardpaste soup bowls seem at first a combination of Chinese Export and Meissen.

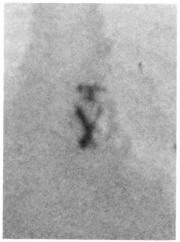

The bottom marks combine crossed swords or are they an X and a T? Or is it a false mark for a Chinese Export piece? Judged on the basis of style and decoration, the bowl appears to be late-18th-century.

A set of small *hardpaste soup bowls* were not so easy to identify. At first glance, they seemed a combination of Chinese Export and Meissen. The acorn knob topping the lids was similar to that on many 18th-century pieces. The use of an animal head as a handle, with the bowl as a body gave the piece an Oriental feeling. The bottom marks were a combination of crossed swords or an *X* and a *T*. After thumbing through hundreds of marks, the closest I could come were those of a potter who had worked for the Meissen factory at one time and had used similar marks, but it wasn't close enough. Could this perhaps be a false mark done by the Chinese for export to Europe and therefore a false clue? The best clues were the materials in the piece (hardpaste porcelain), the design (Export), and the similarity to Meissen pieces. Judging it by the style of decoration, I would date it as late-18th-century.

Among the highest priced *glassware* these days is anything with Tiffany, Steuben, or Frederick Carder signatures. Their highly stylized work, most of which is signed, is pretty easy to spot. You can recognize Aurene luster, or *verre de soie* without even looking for a signature. But if the piece in question had a paper label, long since disintegrated, how do you identify it? Some Tiffany and Steuben ware did have paper labels. To add to the confusion, these companies had their imitators, both in the United States and in Europe.

One of the few pieces of glassware left at a housesale was a small green dish with the look of opal glass. Two sides of the dish were pulled up and the handles were in the shape of dolphins. The center of the dish had a small, round hollowed-out center. The color closely resembled jade green. Held up to the light, the dish seemed almost transparent. There seemed to be no distinguishing marks whatsoever.

Assumption 1: Because it is so perfectly proportioned, it was probably made in the early 20th century. The style isn't of the late-19th-century art glass. If it was any earlier than that, it would have been handmade.

Assumption 2: The dolphins were popular design motifs with the Boston and Sandwich Glass Company, used in their late-19th-century colored glass pieces. Can the dish be late art glass after all? The antiques detective must look through books illustrating art glass of the early 20th century. Of course, such a search leads to Tiffany, Frederick Carder, and Steuben glass. One book picturing catalog pages from the Carder designs is especially promising. "Jade Glass" describes the color of the dish. But no dolphin shapes seemed to have been used for anything except compote stems. Reading on, the antiques detective learns that the dish was probably an underplate for a sherbet dish and that many glass companies adopted the jade-green translucent glass technique. While not completely successful, at least the antiques detective has been able to date and identify the material the dish was made from. Then, one day, a glass collector goes over the piece with a strong magnifying glass. Under one handle there is a fleur de lis mark used by Steuben. Who would want to go to all that trouble for one little piece of glass priced at three dollars? An antiques detective who is insatiably curious about his possessions.

Antique dolls are usually marked or have characteristics that make them easy to identify. Since there are almost more doll collectors than any other kind of collector, there is a mad scramble at every sale or auction to discover the marks that earn money for dealers. Among the early-19th-century "most wanted" are those made by Ludwig Greiner. He had the first patent for making papier-mâché dolls in 1858. His "heads" had cloth stuffed noses and chins. His gold and black label is inside the head and therefore a little hard to see, so searchers look for outside characteristics. Royal Kaestner dolls (made in Germany in the early 1900's) are easier to spot, with their mark stamped on their chests. The finest have open mouths, revealing pearly teeth, and eyes that open and shut. Also easy to identify are the

Among the most sought-after dolls are those with the Kaestner mark. This one is a collector's item, with pearly teeth and eyes that open and shut. With the mark stamped on her chest, she's easy to identify.

The famous "crown" stamp is status in the doll collectors' world.

Schoenhut dolls of 1911. The heads were basswood and their carved, patent-ed joints let them sit or stand in a variety of positions. Up until 1919, all had quaint character faces. Some dolls are also identifiable by their numbers. But how do you date and identify a homemade primitive doll, especially if it is black? Simon and Halbig of Germany made far from primitive brown bisque dolls. Ellis and Lue Taylor, who made wooden dolls in the United States in the 1870's and 1880's, made dolls of rock maple, except for their metal hands and feet. These dolls moved in acrobatic positions and some were painted with black faces for special orders.

Quite the opposite of the "marked" doll is a primitive black doll, found on the floor of a housesale.

I saw a black doll lying in front of the fireplace at an estate sale. Dealers picked her up, searched for identity marks, then with a look of disgust and comments like, "too primitive for me," carelessly dropped the doll back on the floor. Even with the price tag of twenty dollars, there were no takers on the second day of the sale. I was fascinated by the obviously hand-carved, black-painted head, combined with white papier-mâché feet and cloth body. She was well-clothed in a new dress, but wore her original red leather shoes and pantaloons. Thinking she would look nice under my Victorian Christmas tree, I took her home where the first thing I did was undress her to look for any marks. I found a very faint stamp on the doll's right arm. In a circle was J.L., 1874. The head and chest were carved from a single piece of wood that fit inside the cloth body. Even the eyes, nose, and mouth were carved from the same piece. The paint on the mouth had almost worn off. The hair was painted black, as were the eyes.

Clue 1: The cloth body with papier-mâché feet probably once contained a papier-mâché head of white complexion. When the original head became damaged, the doll was probably handed down to the black servants' children. Refitted with a black carved head, the doll was partially changed to suit a new owner.

Clue 2: Research shows that J.L. was Jacob Lacmann, a business associate of Ludwig Greiner who was an American doll maker. Lacmann made bodies only in the 1870's.

Clue 3: The leather boots and pantaloons were fashionable in the late 19th century. Since dolls followed fashion trends when new, clothing is a strong clue.

Deduction: It can probably be classified as a primitive since the head is hand-carved and attached to a more formal doll body. Since the head is made from maple, a wood native to America, the origin, at least judging by the head, is American. You know the body is also American from the stamp. The doll dates from the late 19th century and has a value of over four hundred dollars.

For an antiques detective, that was a relatively easy doll to identify. Much harder are current reproductions of Jenny Lind dolls with hand-decorated porcelain heads or the brand-new Bye-Lo babies. The antiques detective would think twice before buying a Bye-Lo doll for one hundred or more dollars when the dealer pays four and a half dollars right off the assembly line.

Would you pass by a handsome *soup tureen* in the shape of, say, a swan or an animal head just because it had no marks? You might pass up a priceless Meissen or Chinese antique if you did. While most such fantastic treasures are behind museum glass, the antiques detective will always anticipate finding such rarities. To prepare for the possibility, he will familiarize himself with the various materials, shapes, and appearance of early 18th-century ceramics. Sometimes there never were any marks, or the mark has worn away. The antiques detective would send away for the color catalog of

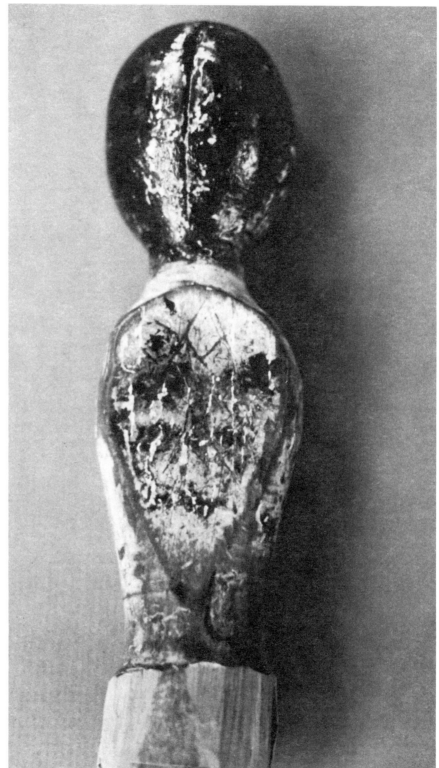

The first step in searching for clues to identity is to take her apart. As you can see, the head and chest are one solid carved piece of maple.

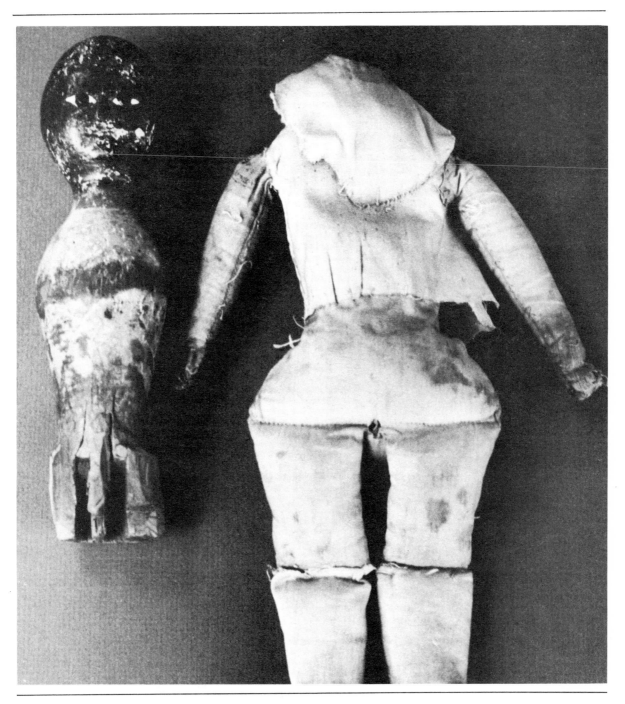

Poor baby, she looks pretty primitive without her fancy clothes. Notice now the cloth body and white papier-mâché hands. Was she originally a white doll that changed color at the hands of a woodcarver?

The Campbell Museum Collection, Camden, New Jersey. While the objects pictured are primarily soup tureens, many examples of 18th-century hard-paste porcelain and other fine ceramic pieces are pictured along with their marks. Even more helpful are the pictures of the pieces without marks. The Chinese adapted animal-head designs from the Europeans and turned them into Chinese Export porcelain. You can see that the animal heads are strictly Oriental in feeling.

For many years I have been living with a "tazza," a deep flat dish on a single foot. It was one of the numerous things I inherited from my late mother-in-law, a dedicated antique collector. Not being an antiques detective, she bought what struck her fancy, but if it had no marks to identify it, she didn't bother to find out anything about it. Once, when I had asked her about the piece, she had said she thought it was possibly majolica of some sort, maybe Italian or Spanish. As you can see, it is either crudely made or maybe just suffering from extreme age. The floral pattern is in bluish-green and yellows. There are no marks whatsoever on it. A closeup of the "coat of arms" which is in the center of the dish shows bright red balls. About fifteen years ago I decided to take my tazza to an antique show that offered appraisals as part of the come-on. Two experts told me without hesitation that it was Mexican, made in the 1920's. Somehow, their appraisal didn't seem right. I began studying book after book and visiting ceramic exhibits in museums. Could it be Chinese Export from a titled family? It had the same heavy look as some of the earthenware pieces made for export. But the finish was not the same nor was the floral design in keeping with such 18th-century pieces. Observation of similar finishes taught me it was called "polychrome." It resembled some pieces of early Delft and English Delftware. By mere chance I spotted a book, *Collecting European Delft and Faience,* by Diana Imber.

This "tazza" has no identifying marks. Notice the crudeness of the foot. Would you recognize it as middle-19th-century French Faience?

Is this a family crest? It is more likely a guild coat of arms, popular at the time.

Thumbing through it, I saw similar pieces and designs attributed to 18th-century French Faience. I read that heraldic motifs were used at Moustiers, France. The floral borders copied the earlier designs begun at Rouen, France. Until I see a closely related piece otherwise authenticated, I shall label my tazza as middle-18th-century French Faience, possibly from Rouen or Moustiers. As to the heraldic coat of arms, it could be a guild symbol, from fishmonger to who-knows-what? Some day when I have a free moment, I'll determine that in a book describing 18th-century guilds.

Another of my mother-in-law's finds was quite a mystery until recently. A silver set of "fish" knives and forks went unrecognized until I purchased a small paperback book, *Bradbury's Book of Hallmarks.* I had already been through the big, fat books on English silver plate and American silver

Study this closeup of the mark on a silver knife. The crossed keys in combination with crown and date letters identified a fish set of Sheffield plate.

marks, to no avail. Only one clue, the crown mark on the handle, had told me the pieces were English. Yet there were no lions, leopards, George or Victoria heads, all marks for British silver plate. In addition to the crown, the pieces had crossed keys and a diamond with date letters enclosed. At the end of Bradbury's book, in the section on "Old Sheffield Plate Makers' Marks," I found my crown combined with crossed key hallmarks. Under the category "Group III," was mention of forks, dessert knives, etc., plated with "thin sheets of silver attached thereto by solder; this process was described as 'close plating.' As the origin of this method was associated with the town of Birmingham, it will be found that a great influx of makers' marks was registered in Sheffield by the producers of Close Plate in that town in the year 1807." Another paragraph narrowed the possible date to between 1840 and 1860 and noted that the articles so marked were nickel, silver-plated by "the process of electro-deposition." As I have said before, the antiques detective has to have a lot of patience. Somewhere, somehow, every object can eventually be identified.

9.
Sifting
the Evidence

How would you like to spend an evening with a chair leg? If you are truly a dedicated antiques detective this can be the equivalent of a gambler spending an evening at the tables in Vegas. The chair leg in question is no ordinary leg and the stakes are high. The leg may be an appendage of an authentic American easy chair, *circa* 1790, a wing-back. Age may have caused its separation from the rest of the chair and that is what the antiques detective hopes to find out for sure, peering through a magnifying glass and turning the leg in a variety of directions.

I first saw the *wing-back chair* propped against a garage wall, its broken leg tied together with clothesline and the upholstery torn on one side. There should have been a cushioned seat, but there wasn't. The three young women conducting their first garage sale (they said) were doing a terrific business in toys and last year's designer dresses. The house attached to the garage was in the two-hundred-thousand-dollar range and bore an address guaranteed to draw a crowd. The scant pieces of furniture for sale included one fascinating item—an oversized custom-made combination coffee table and hibachi pit for two hundred dollars! There was also a selection of battered chairs. Wearing a sold tag was a handsome birdseye maple chest of drawers. It had been priced at one hundred dollars. The broken wing chair was an obvious loser at five dollars. However, the broken leg caught my attention. Even in the dark corner of the garage, the cabriole leg ending in a ball-and-claw foot was unmistakable. Of course, it was a department store purchase,

141

circa 1920 or 1960, or, perhaps, judging by the fancy surroundings, a custom-made Williamsburg Village copy of a Chippendale chair.

An antiques detective must expect the unexpected. It certainly isn't logical to expect to confront an original Frederic Remington painting in an apartment building's laundry room or an 18th-century Chippendale chair at a suburban garage sale. It is totally unexpected.

But the collector who rules out the unexpected is apt to miss rarities in unlikely places. Accustomed to seeing Depression glass at garage sales, he will doubt his own eyes if an 18th- or early-19th-century piece of glassware sits amid all the Depression glass. After all, haven't all the experts declared in print and on television that these days there simply aren't any pieces of early American or English glass to be found outside of museums and the private collections of the wealthy? Wouldn't these experts and the professional dealers spot such valuable antiques first? Nonsense! The true antiques detective will spot that one-of-a-kind oldie amidst the junk, standing out like a ball-and-claw foot.

Meanwhile, back at the garage sale, an antique dealer who was busy packing up the Depression glass found my intent scrutiny of the wing chair amusing. In a loud voice she jeered, "Ho! Ho! Looks like a ball-and-claw foot. Must be garage Chippendale." As all eyes turned to stare, I reached in my purse for the five dollars. Right or wrong, I had just become the proud owner of a broken chair. Once I got the chair home, I could begin searching for the clues. As I turned to leave, one of the housewives said, "That was a nice chair. It belonged to my grandmother. When she died we planned to have it fixed, but never got around to it. Besides, that broken leg keeps coming off even with the metal braces we hammered on."

Once home, I wrestled to remove the clothesline. Off came the leg and out came my magnifying glass. Setting the leg aside, I began my investigation with the complete silhouette of the chair. The wings were graceful and the arms turned outward in a *C* scroll. Though the seat looked higher than on authentic chairs of this type, this could only be determined after the upholstery was partially removed. An antiques detective can't really know any upholstered piece until it has been stripped to the bare bones. The legs were of mahogany, cabriole with raised scroll carving on the sides adjacent to the knee. The feet held a flattened ball and the knuckles of the foot were quite distinct and angular. From top to bottom the chair was forty-six inches high. If I ignored the 1920's fabric covering the chair, it outwardly appeared to be Chippendale-style. My next step was to check the leg out clue by clue.

Clue 1: The carving on the foot and leg appeared to have been done by hand. The leg was joined to the seat rail with wooden pegs or dowels which were partially broken off.

Clue 2: The saw marks visible on the top of the leg had a slight arc-like curve.

Clue 3: Plane marks on the inside curved surface of the leg were obvious as thin, ripple marks, a sign of the machine planer, in general use after the 1830's.

Would you pass up this wing-back chair with its 1920's ragged covering? Would you even consider that it might be older than it looks?

This closeup of the leg shows the cabriole with raised scroll carving on the sides, the ball-and-claw foot.

Deduction: These three clues practically tell the date of this chair. The construction discussed in Clue 1 is typical of middle-19th-century work, even though mortising machines that placed the dowels in furniture were in use by the early part of the 19th century. The usual Chippendale-style chair leg was extended into the dovetail form, up through the chair rail and held firmly with a mortise and tenon joint on either side. Clue 2 reveals circular saw marks that put the chair into the 19th century, because the circular saw didn't come into use until after the 1830's. Of course, wherever these dates are concerned, there are always exceptions. Not every cabinetmaker threw away his old tools the minute a new gizmo came along. Therefore, a chair or other piece of furniture might have been made later than the tool marks would indicate.

The hard-working antiques detectives has to come to many more deductions before a final statement is made on the wing-back. Slashing and ripping at the already torn upholstery, I laid bare one arm and the front seat rail. Ankle deep in cotton stuffing and horsehair, I wrenched out upholstery tacks until one side of the chair was stripped to the secondary wood. You might wonder what is so important about what's under the stuffing. Who would ever see it anyway?

Clue 4: The front section of the seat rail was birdseye maple. The side rail was pine, as was the arm construction. The base of the arm had a curved piece of red oak attached, to give an outward swirl to the bottom of the arm.

Clue 5: The red oak section showed the old hand saw marks.

Clue 6: A hand-forged "rose head" nail was removed from the inside section of the rail seat.

Deduction: Birdseye maple was prominently used as early as 1815 and, like pine, is a native American wood. The hand-forged nail isn't really a clue to age in this case. The marks of the handsaw on the oak arm attachment can also be discounted; the saw may simply have been handy when the piece needed to be made. Based on all the above information and clues, I deduced that the chair is American-made after the middle of the 19th century, possibly even as late as 1876 when the Centennial was celebrated by a revival of 18th-century furnishings.

The five-dollar chair isn't worth the four thousand dollars it could have brought if it had been authentic 1700's, but you'd have to pay at least five hundred dollars for it in an antique shop. If it could pass the scrutiny of experts at auction that's quite a profit and the chances are it would.

Early American country style furniture is relatively simple for the antiques detective to identify. Once you know what you are looking for, the saw marks are easy to see and the marks left by the hand-turned lathe are quite evident in the authentic pieces. Just try to find them on the beautifully finished fakes! Candlestands are among the most popular items with both collectors and fakers.

Note the circular saw marks on a broken cross section of the block supporting a leg.

A section of the arm from the side shows circular saw marks on the arm support.

The arm and support laid bare show two kinds of wood and saw marks that appear to be modern. Other marks show that this section is newer than others and was probably used for repair.

*An antiques detective could rec-
ognize the lines of a hand-turned
candlestand, even when painted
black.*

A closeup shows the manner in which the legs are dovetailed into the pedestal, as well as plane marks.

The *candlestand* you see here was painted black and was being used as a telephone stand in an apartment. Black-enameled furniture doesn't do much for me and I almost passed it by. I had answered an ad for a quilt, which turned out to be a disappointment. As I turned to leave, I finally spotted the small black candlestand. By instinct I saw it in silhouette, without embellishments. Even with a coat of black paint, there was a hand-turned look to its central pedestal. Specks of gilt gleamed through the animal-shaped feet. When I picked up the table, I could see that under the black paint, the feet were probably brass. I very carefully removed the black paint. What emerged was a charming, two-tiered walnut candlestand. The legs were dovetailed into the pedestal. Plane marks on the base indicated its date of manufacture to be about 1830. It could have been a holdover from the Duncan Phyfe period (1810–20). It is definitely a handmade, hand-turned stand, but whether for candles or food, who can say?

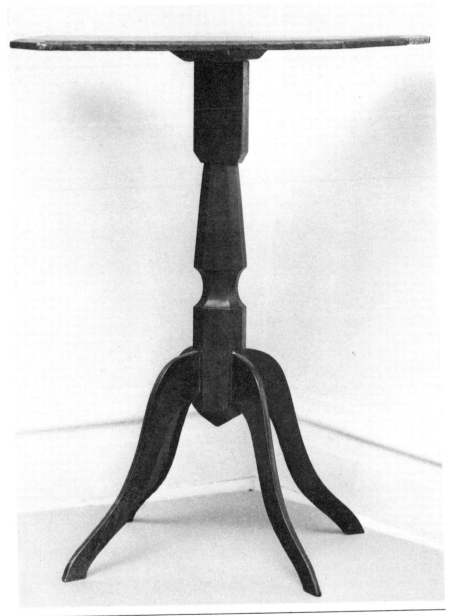

You can recognize the lines of an early-19th-century candlestand, even in profile.

Here is a true candlestand. Judge it by its silhouette and you see classic form in a country piece. Turned upside down, you'll find a clue to its age in the cross cleat glued to the top tenon of the stem. It is similar to the simple Shaker designs and might even be a Shaker piece. If so, it may have been done in the West, since tables there were made of walnut, as this one is. The curved legs are cut on the bias of the wood so that the grain follows parallel to the curve. The Shaker workmen did this to prevent splitting. Found at a conducted housesale in the Midwest, it dates from the early 19th century and is quite a find for twenty dollars.

Note the curved legs cut on the bias of the wood and the cross cleat glued to the top tenon of the stem.

What's wrong with this chest? It looks very old, but what are those blocks of wood doing on the top of the ball feet?

Should your best friend be told she has spent three hundred dollars for a "married" piece, especially when she loves every faked inch of it? Knowing her penchant for antique English oak pieces, her decorator came right over with a so-called "17th-century" chest of drawers. Now she has invited you to see and celebrate the new purchase. You have become pretty good at identifying antiques. Does this oak chest really look like a 17th-century English oak piece? At first glance it seems properly ancient, in fact, downright battered. Look at the bottom of the piece. What are those blocks of wood between the base and the feet? They aren't even the same color as the rest of the chest. The entire piece looks squooshed together, especially the ball feet. Scrutinize the vertical moulding on the sides of the chest. It is a most unusual double moulding or a new body built around an old chest. A look at the back of the chest explains all.

The photo of the back shows that two separate pieces have been put together. Notice the lighter color of the two cut-out pieces of wood near the top. This apparently is where two hinges were once fastened. The top at one time lifted up. The upper section of the piece could originally have been a blanket chest. The two small drawers at the top could have been dummies. The top and the bottom are extremely wobbly, like a couple of orange crates glued together. In order to hold the entire thing together, the faker built a frame around two different pieces. The patination on the carcass and back frame is darker than the supposed back of the drawers. There are a few early nailheads protruding.

A look at the back reveals that two different pieces of furniture have been put together. Notice the two light rectangles at each end that tell the antiques detective there were once two hinges attached and the top lifted up. Perhaps this was once a blanket chest?

A closeup of the shell of the drawer shows it is correctly made for ca. 1670.

Clue 1: Where are the crude marks of the pit saw? On a piece this primitive, such saw marks should certainly be visible. On the left top side, the easily apparent arc lines made by a circular saw erase two hundred years.

Clue 2: The sides of the drawers have the proper coarse dovetails at the front. The butted back and the runners made to fit in grooved sides are correct for the period. However, the drawers show no early saw marks. Circular lines are faintly visible.

Clue 3: The base of the chest with wood blocks supporting ball feet provides the most obvious clue that something funny is going on. Even turning the chest upside down, you'll never know what type of feet or base, or if any, rightfully belonged to the original chest.

Clue 4: The price is another clue. While three hundred dollars is cheap for an authentic English 17th-century chest, it is also too much to pay for a flimsily made fake. If you ever get stuck with something like this, you'd better have a sense of humor, especially when it totally collapses like a house of cards when someone accidentally bangs the vacuum into it.

It's much more fun to buy an authentic late-17th- or 18th-century bed that everybody thinks is a 19th-century country piece. Bought "in the rough" during the closing hours of a conducted housesale for eighty dollars, my weathered gray bed has blossomed into a handsome walnut beauty. Shown in the rough is the headboard, which is identical to the footboard.

The hand-turnings on the headboard with an 18th-century rope bed show up even though the bed is "in the rough." They provide enough clues to the antiques detective, along with the style of the spindles, to date the bed from somewhere in the late 17th or early 18th century.

In this detail of a bed spindle, note the concentric lines showing hand-turning and the split-turning, typical of late 17th- or early 18th-century decorative details.

Not shown are recently made side rails. Try a little *déjà-vu* on this one. Where have you seen bedposts with this bold ring-turning and finials? Does the contrast of delicate baluster spindles remind you of something similar? Do the words "Brewster chair" come to mind? I know it sounds impossible, but isn't everything in the antique world improbable? The Brewster chair, *circa* 1640 to early 18th century, is usually on display in museums in the East. Most originated in and around Massachusetts. Of the earliest *rope-bed style,* there are no pegs to help secure the rope.

Before I carried the bed away, I asked the sellers if they knew anything about it. It had been purchased in Massachusetts at a country auction a long time ago. The owners had gotten as far as having it stripped and then had given up.

Lots of elbow grease and Wattco, a commercial Danish furniture-finishing preparation which gives wood a natural rather than a super-glossy shellacked look, eventually rubbed up a beautiful, dark walnut color. That early craftsman had quite a talent. Centered in each of the horizontal bed rail spindles is exquisitely grained oystering. Nobody in my household has enough pioneer spirit to weave a clothesline mattress for the bed and so, instead we use it as twin headboards. A great number of experts have looked at the bed and not believed it was of such an early vintage, which is undoubtedly why it was passed up at the housesale. No one expected to find a late-17th-century bed in the Midwest, much less at a housesale, priced so low. I have seen only one other similar bed, at one of the better antique shows, priced at nine hundred dollars. Its monetary value isn't nearly as important to me as the pleasure that I can derive from living with and studying the craftsmanship of an early American rope bed.

Clue 1: Not only does the antiques detective look for telltale concentric lines of the hand-operated lathe on any piece supposedly of the 17th or 18th century, but the style of the turnings further dates a piece. The lathe marks also help authenticate it. The first clue to the age of this bed is the manner in which the posts and spindles are turned. The heavy posts show split-turning, typical of late-17th-century American furniture.

Clue 2: The decorative spindles are similar to the type illustrated in the Wallace Nutting book, *Checklist of Early American Reproductions.* One of the Nutting reproductions of a Brewster bed, No. 811, is a refined version of this more primitive piece.

Clue 3: The use of oystering as a method of bringing out the natural beauty of the wood as a decoration, rather than ornate carving, is typical of the 17th and 18th century. The oval-shaped designs were made by using cross sections of roots and branches. In this instance, the effect was achieved by crosscutting the wood itself.

Clue 4: The absence of the pegs as well as holes in the head and footboard needed for the usual rope bed indicate a type of pegless roping common in the late-17th- and early-18th-century country pieces.

Clue 5: The marks of the handsaw or pit saw help date the piece as 17th- or 18th-century.

Deduction: The piece is American, probably early-18th-century. Since fashions moved and changed slowly in remote sections of the American countryside, the piece may be later than the design indicates. It is probably from Massachusetts, since that area is where the type originated.

Another totally unexpected discovery was that of two early low-back *Windsor chairs* at the local furniture stripping shop, which was selling out, including unclaimed pieces he had already removed the paint from. I walked past a long row of chairs and tables with the grey, furred look that comes from a rough chemical bath. At first glance, they all looked pretty much the same, the common variety of country plank-bottom chairs. As I stared at them collectively, two shapes suddenly stood out from the others. Pointing, I asked, "How much for those two with the arms?" Looking surprised at my choice, he said, "Four dollars each, lady. But wouldn't you rather buy something else? Those two are in pretty bad shape."

Handing him the eight dollars, I hauled the chairs into the light of day. (Incidentally, much of an antiques detective's life is spent hauling objects from place to place.) The "stripper" was right. In the bright sunlight the chairs looked pretty awful. Several of the spindles were loose and one was cracked. Nevertheless, they appeared to be handmade, low-backed Windsor chairs. The larger of the two had ring-turned spindles and a back-sweeping crest rail. When I turned them over, the underside of the crest rail revealed that the top attached to the spindles with pegs. The marks on both the seat bottoms, even in their sorry state, showed the unmistakably jagged marks of an 18th-century frame saw. Legs, stretchers, and arm spindles all had the concentric rings of the hand-turned lathe. The seats on both chairs were almost two inches thick.

Clue: Several clues instantly date the chairs to the late 18th or early 19th century: the tool marks, the thick ring-turning, thickness of seats, and peg construction.

After several days of hand sanding with both sandpaper and No. 00 steel wool, the wood grain and color began to appear. It's not easy to sand or steel wool turned pieces. When they were smooth enough, I gave both pieces the first coat of Wattco. The smaller of the two chairs on page 159 has a seat and horseshoe-shaped arms of walnut. The crest rail is hickory. The legs and spindles are oak. In shape, with only slightly angled legs, it is probably English. Horseshoe-shaped arms are usually found in this style of English chair. Some initials on the bottom of the seat are barely visible. The ring-turned chair on page 158 is made of the same kinds of wood as the other chair. Except for the fact that ring turnings are usually an American style, I would say it was English.

Deduction: Both chairs are probably middle-19th-century English or American.

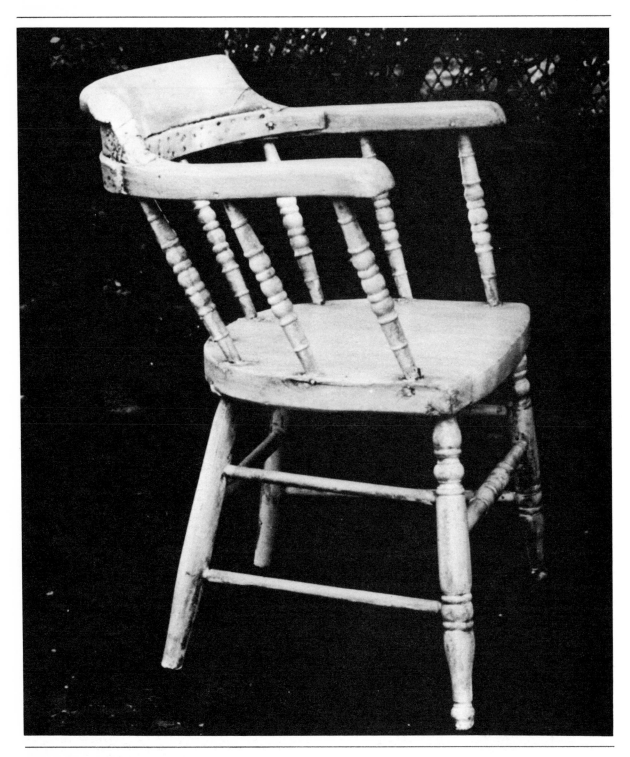

This profile of a ring-turned low-back Windsor chair in a rough state reveals where repairs have been made on the back.

You can learn more about the construction of the chairs by looking under the crest rail. Note the use of wooden pegs.

I would like to interject a footnote at this point to reveal a crime committed in the strip shop. A short time later I returned to the stripper's to find some other unclaimed antiques. Though I found nothing, as I was leaving, I saw two workmen moving a massive high chest of drawers that seemed to date from around the middle of the 18th century. The striking thing about it was the japanned finish. As the name implies, japanning imitated the lacquered furniture of the Orient and was a popular form of decorating furniture, especially around Boston and New York, till almost the end of the 18th century. The decorations of birds, flowers and people were raised from the surface on the fine city-made pieces. The background was tortoise shell or black. Needless to say, there aren't too many in the antique marketplace. The fragile nature of the process makes it costly to repair those that have survived. Seeing one of these rarities heading for the chemical vats left me almost speechless with horror. In what must have been a loud voice I shouted, "You can't strip that piece!" I did everything but put my arms around the chest to protect it from its fate. The startled workmen halted momentarily, and then continued. "We got a job to do, lady. This is what we get paid for." "At least give me the name of the owner before you strip it," I begged. "Perhaps he or she doesn't realize what this piece is worth with even the missing paint." They shrugged. "It's———Antique Shop," they said. That was astounding. An antique dealer would surely know such a japanned piece was too rare to strip! I dashed to the pay phone. The dealer did indeed know what the piece was. "If you want to save it so badly, pay me thirteen thousand dollars and it's all yours. Otherwise, I'm stripping it to the pine base and selling it for eight thousand at the Lake Forest Antique Show." Sadly, I declined the offer. The dealer had shown the piece in the shop for a long time. Preferring to turn a fast buck, she destroyed a piece of rare American furniture. At the next Lake Forest Antique Show, I stopped at her booth and saw the stripped chest marked eight thousand dollars. Even as I stood there, it was purchased. Though the new owner didn't know that her piece had once been a masterpiece of American cabinet making, I believe if she had seen the chest in its original condition, she would still have purchased it. If she could afford eight thousand, what's thirteen?

As we know, antiques have their fashions and fads. Many early-19th-century antiques are consistently passed up, even with cheap price tags, simply because they aren't "in." Federal mirrors and stipple prints, once the ultimate in décor, can hardly be given away at housesales. I don't mean just the obvious mirrors that combine gilt with carved eagles. It is entirely possible to pick up a rectangular gilt mirror of the Federal period for twenty dollars. I bought one by accident. I went to a conducted housesale in an old Victorian house, to look for brass fire dogs. The ad had said there would be some. After standing in the usual long line and being pushed through the doors, I headed straight for the fireplace. I took a quick look at the andirons and dashed to the seller's table. "Hold the andirons for me, I want to look around." My primary mission accomplished, I hurried back into the living

room and noticed the mirror above the fireplace. It was a typical three-paneled Federal mirror with reeded cornices. What caught my eye, however, were the neo-classical prints inside the two end panels. Coming closer and using my magnifying glass, I could make out the faint signature: "After Angelica Kauffmann; Francesco Bartolozzi engraver." Now it became a simple mattero of *déjà-vu* taking over, because I had seen these prints before. The Greek mythological figures of Venus and Cupid had been painted by Angelica Kauffmann in the 18th century as murals for a royal household. Kauffmann was famed as a painter during the Adam period. English architect, Robert Adam, brought about a revival in neo-classical furniture around the middle of the 18th century. Kauffmann carried out the themes with painted furniture, small enamels, and wall and ceiling murals. Bartolozzi came along later to make engravings of her most famous paintings. A status symbol of the early 19th century was a Bartolozzi engraving. I recalled one book's saying that the most fashionable American homes of that period had Hepplewhite's "new designs" and Angelica Kauffmann engravings by Bartolozzi. You can hardly give away one of these prints today, even if it is *circa* 1800. Does this tell you something about today's status symbol furnishings?

The mirror, including the two engravings, was priced at twenty-two dollars, probably about the same as it cost when it was fashionable in 1800 and not much of an investment appreciation.

Returning to the checkout table, I encountered an enraged dealer who had hoped to buy my andirons, especially for twenty dollars. She was holding a set of brass fire tools. "They go with your andirons, the seller told me." No wonder the dealer was sore! To rub it in, I tapped the andirons with my pen and they rang like a bell. They turned out to be of fine brass, made around 1800.

10. Mistaken Identity

> *I had come to an erroneous conclusion which shows, my dear Watson, how dangerous it always is to reason from insufficient data.*
>
> —SHERLOCK HOLMES,
> in *The Adventure of the Speckled Band*

You'd be surprised how many cases of mistaken identity there are in the antiques world, even though most of us are more sophisticated than the antique collectors of twenty years ago. It can happen to anyone, from collector to museum curator. One person's mistake can be another's discovery. It still amazes me though how many collectors become totally naïve at a country auction. They act as though they never saw an antique before. Who can resist the lure of a full-color auction catalog of supposedly Early American country antiques, especially when the auction is held in the heartland of country Americana—Wild Goose, Vermont. Doesn't that name "Wild Goose, Vermont," reek of folksy antiques? If you love country pieces and primitives, you probably mail away for all the promising color catalogs from the East. When you begin to go through them and see closeup pictures of battered tilt-top tables, country Sheraton pine, and maple dressing tables with original paint, it becomes even more enchanting. But use your magnifying glass to look at the close-up photos, where the underside of the piece is showing. It may be that perennial favorite, the shoe-foot chair-table or the underside of a tilt table, both supposedly 18th-century. Even without a magnifying glass, it is easy to see that the tilt table hasn't warped in two hundred years despite its battered surface and scarred feet. If the table is that beaten-up, shouldn't the wood have shrunk a little? With the magnifying glass, you also look for tool marks but see no rough saw marks. Amazing, too, how well-preserved the "original" paint finish is on that handsomely painted

Sheraton dressing table. Even more amazing is that you saw one just like it in an antique shop in your own neighborhood, as much a twin as if it had been painted on an assembly line, but of course, that couldn't be. Wild Goose is a thousand miles away. If you decide to take your camper to the Wild Goose auction, glazed eyeball syndrome may cause you to forget all reason. There is so much to bid on and it is all so charming and quaint. Before you know it, for a bargain price of three hundred dollars you are the proud owner of a dressing table. People are congratulating you for your spirited bids that beat out that dealer from the East. Flushed with success, you cart the piece fifteen hundred miles to your home to discover the dressing table not only isn't 19th-century, but probably isn't even early-20th. You accepted it as an authentic piece without looking beyond the fancy paint job. Be glad you didn't buy the "authentic 18th-century foot-chair table." This high-backed arm chair has a round table top attached to its chair back. What the catalog describes as "old red paint" means paint that has been sitting around for as much as a year waiting for the cabinetmaker to finish the "authentic foot-chair table." By the time you see it, there will doubtless be pine knotholes showing through the properly cracked paint or the piece may be finished in odious orange shellac to accentuate the pine knots. In either event, you would make a mistake identifying this as other than "authentic 20th-century fake." When such cutesy, quasi-quaint pieces turn up at country auctions, enraptured collectors stop examining the piece at the first sight of a pine knothole. They see only the overall design and not the minute details. For years these pieces have been big sellers on the country auction circuit and as long as no one bothers to check them out, clue by clue, they'll continue to sell. You wouldn't have one in your country kitchen, would you?

If it will make you feel any better, I too have a case of "mistaken identity" sitting in my garage. If it sits there long enough, it will at least be a respectable reproduction. It remains exactly as I found it many years ago, in rotten shape. As you can see, it has a few things missing, such as a drawer and door. That broken board on the floor in the foreground was once the "bottle drawer." Thinking I had made a valuable discovery, I snapped this picture of the sideboard where I found it in the basement of a a rattle-trap frame mansion. I have come to realize that not everything that comes out of mansions is worth taking. I was led off the track by the many pieces of Empire and early Victorian furniture in this particular house. Wondering why there were so many once fine antiques with missing legs or bashed-in cabinet doors, I asked their owner. "I had six sons and I wanted them to grow up living with fine antiques, but boys will be boys." Pulling out the writing leaf on a once beautiful antique desk she showed me two carved hearts and initials. "My youngest did that when he was just twelve years old. Today he's a professional artist. That's why I never had it refinished. It may be valuable someday." As for the Hepplewhite sideboard, she was willing to let it go for fifty dollars. She remembered buying it twenty years ago from one of the finest antique shops in the city. Somewhere she had papers that said it was authentic. "This was quite a rarity you know," she said. "It came from

At first glance, this piece looks like a Hepplewhite sideboard. If it were authentic, it would be worth buying for fifty dollars even in this rotten condition.

the south, where they had bottle or wine drawers. You can probably fix this drawer easily." I was impressed, but I did wish that the basement was better lighted. The piece looked correct in its outline form. When I pulled one of the drawers out to examine the dovetailing, it was very nicely done. The fact that the bottom of the drawer was very smooth could be accounted for. It wouldn't be out of place to replace a drawer bottom in a hundred or more years' time. I could just make out the handsome banding and inlays that were fairly intact on the drawers and legs. The veneer top might have to be replaced, but the general finish would respond to some good polishing. Self-confidently, I paid her the fifty dollars and made arrangements for delivery. I was so excited at finding an authentic Hepplewhite sideboard, even in bad shape, that I ignored my better judgment. Because I wanted it to be authentic, it had to be authentic.

Upon examining it in full daylight, I felt a little sick. What looked old in the dark looked like a reproduction *circa* 1940 in daylight.

Clue 1: The ends of the drawer sides, at the dovetailing, had been rubbed with a brownish stain to simulate age. There were no marks of tools or old nails whatsoever on the bottom of the drawer.

Clue 2: Peering inside the case, I looked for any tool marks, but by then I knew it was hopeless. On the back of the piece I found two branded initials and several numbers. I phoned the shop where the former owner had purchased the sideboard. Explaining I had just bought a piece purchased from their gallery, I asked if they knew whose initials were on the back. With candor and a touch of pride, the dealer told me, "Why, he was one of our top furniture reproduction men. He specialized in Hepplewhite sideboards. They were correct to the last detail. If you didn't know, you would certainly believe they were authentic antiques."

Some of the worst cases of mistaken identity occur at professionally conducted housesales. "We know what we are selling," is the universal chant. "We have had everything examined by experts." There is that word *experts* again! To the antiques detective this is good news. It means he has a better than fifty-fifty chance of finding an underpriced rarity at one of these sales. Every antiques detective is aware that these days experts are coming out of the woodwork to appraise and authenticate everything from your beer cans to your phony Chippendale chairs. Yes, there really is an expert who specializes in beer can appraisals. He gets his information from the books published by other beer can collectors, who hope to raise the ante on their collections. There is also an appraiser who specializes in such "new antiques" as Fiesta ware and Barbie dolls. My favorite appraisers are those who run mail-order appraising services or perhaps the expert who takes his typewriter along on house calls to do on-the-spot appraisals and authentications. He has built up quite a following of fans who think his knowledge of old cherry pitters and golden oak is simply amazing. The antiques detective would tell you there is just one small thing wrong with fast-buck appraising. While many antiques and near-antiques can be identified almost instantly

A closeup of the brass shows it has proper period basket-weave design. However, the drawer pull doesn't have the Hepplewhite shape; it is the later Sheraton shape and is not cast, but pressed.

A side view of the drawer shows an evenness of dovetailing that can only be machine-made. Though you can't see it here, the dovetailing on the front has been stained to simulate age. Compare the smooth finish both inside and out with that of the drawers on the Hepplewhite chest-on-chest in Chapter 2.

with only superficial knowledge, the vast majority requires time-consuming research. If you want a real case of mistaken identity, consider a Meissen vase. When our instant appraiser sees the vase and spots the characteristic Meissen crossed swords, he proclaims, "You have Meissen!" Unlike the antiques detective, he doesn't elaborate as to what the date of the Meissen piece is. Unless he has memorized the hundreds of marks used by Meissen to designate dates from 1710 right up through the 1900's, as well as the many similar marks of copiers, his appraisal is all but worthless. Worse yet, the poor victim can now hardly wait to take the bowl to the local auction house. She envisions hundreds of dollars flowing into her straitened bank account. She doesn't know that there is a world of difference in the price of a piece of Meissen marked with crossed swords (1763) and termed "Kings' Period" and that of a piece marked with a set of two crossed swords with intersecting parallel lines, this latter mark meaning the piece was found defective by the factory. An antiques detective would save his money and invest it in a copy of *Marks and Designs,* by William Chaffers. The reliable appraiser, of which there are many, would either do a quick sketch of the marks or take a Polaroid picture and then do some research in the *Marks* book. Like so many others, Meissen is a magic name in the antique business. To the unknowing collector, anything with Meissen marks means money. To the antiques detective it is instead a cause for suspicion. Other magic names that alarm the antiques detective are Staffordshire pottery, Queen Anne furniture, and Ming vases, a brief sampling of the many magic names that have been faked and reproduced over the years. The antiques detective will ignore the names and face the facts. If he's lucky, he'll come up with clues and deductions that will definitely identify the objects. But some marks seem to defy identification.

I am reminded of one of my five-dollar-and-under discoveries at conducted housesales. Because not everybody recognizes an early-19th-century snuff box, I was able to purchase one for five dollars. After numerous dealers had pawed through the jewelry boxes at one housesale, I spotted the leftover

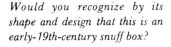

Would you recognize by its shape and design that this is an early-19th-century snuff box?

wooden box. The pickers and dealers apparently thought it was a cheap wooden pill box. As you can see, it has the rectangular shape peculiar to snuff boxes, not ring or pill boxes. The handcarving is obvious in the photograph. An antique shop could sell it for forty-five dollars.

This drawing was sold as American folk art for twenty-five dollars at another conducted housesale. It was drawn with colored pencils on medium-weight paper with an English watermark.

Clue 1: If the drawing had really been done during the era of the steamships (from early to late 19th century), it is doubtful that colored pencils would have been the medium.

Something isn't quite authentic in this pencil drawing sold as antique American folk art. Among other things, the script (printing) is strictly 20th-century.

Clue 2: The script is done in the style or method of the 20th century, not the stylized script taught in the 19th century. The letters of the printed words have a distinctly modern look.

Clue 3: Research into both English and American steamships of the period does not turn up any steamship named *Commodore*.

Deduction: The drawing is a charming attempt to copy the look of folk art. It was probably done in the 1930's to go with antique furnishings. It is, however, "folk art," and as such, is worth the twenty-five-dollar price.

If you contrast that drawing with the oil painting of steamships, you can recognize that the latter is truly a fine example of the "naïve" style. While it first appears as if a child had done it, the perspective is mature; the army tents in the background gradually become larger towards the foreground. This primitive was executed in the middle 19th century when steamships were used to carry supplies to army troops. An antiques detective found it in an attic and purchased it for around seventy-five dollars. Today it might easily bring two hundred fifty to three hundred fifty dollars at a city auction.

Oil painting in the "naïve" style. The steamship identifies it as a middle-19th-century work. Found in an attic by an antiques detective, today it could bring several hundred dollars at an auction.

The facsimile newspaper reads:

THE [Nº 80
New-England Courant.

From MONDAY February 4. to MONDAY February 11. 1723.

Can you imagine finding a rare American newspaper published by a young Benjamin Franklin in a dresser drawer? One day while I was discussing a current exhibit of artifacts of Franklin and Jefferson with a collector, she suddenly leaped out of her chair and said, "Why, do you know I have an old newspaper that says, 'published by Benjamin Franklin' in my bedroom, in one of the drawers? I wonder if it's worth anything!'' After several minutes, she returned carrying a small newspaper framed in a glass and pewter frame. ''It's been in the family so long, I just never think about it,'' she said. Dated 1723, this copy of the *New England Courant* appeared to be genuine and represented the first newspaper printing done by Benjamin Franklin on his own. Significantly, the opening paragraph declares this to be the first issue by the new publisher, Benjamin Franklin. My friend has since checked auction prices and estimates the present value of the newspaper to be between fifteen hundred and several thousand dollars. It's permanently out of the drawer and prominently displayed on a wall. But for our chance conversation, she might have forgotten the historic newspaper stuffed in the drawer and have eventually sold the chest to another collector. It might have been you.

Now that you know all the secrets of this antiques detective, I expect to see at least half of you prowling the next fancy antique show. The other half should be hidden under a Queen Anne chest or tavern table. Is there some little clue you're overlooking? Move over a bit and make room for me!

Index